# FIELD EXPERIENCE IN POSTSECONDARY EDUCATION:

# A Guidebook For Action

**Ernest M. Schuttenberg**
and
**Brent W. Poppenhagen**
**The Cleveland State University**

University Press
of America™

To Ann and Zona

**University Press of America,® Inc.**

4720 Boston Way
Lanham, MD 20706

3 Henrietta Street
London WC2E 8LU England

ISBN:   0-8191-1212-7

Library of Congress Catalog Number:  80-8242

## ACKNOWLEDGMENTS

The authors wish to thank the following persons
for their valuable contributions: Lewis Patterson
and Carol Segebarth for editorial assistance;
Robin Raybuck and Claire Shands for bibliographic
research; and, Enid Bordner and Donna Magri who
prepared the manuscript for publication.

iii

# CONTENTS

# INTRODUCTION

The purpose of this volume is to provide a useful guide for learners and mentors in internship experiences in postsecondary education. The book addresses four main areas within this context: (1) Career Orientation and Planning; (2) Experiential Learning Theory; (3) Individual Learning and Development; and (4) Program Implementation and Evaluation.

While most participants in internship experiences have general career interests, they may hope to refine these interests into more specific career goals during the internship period. Part One of this Guidebook contains an overview of the career possibilities in the areas of instruction, administration, counseling, and support services in postsecondary organizations with educational missions.

In Part Two, several models of field-based learning derived from adult education research are presented and discussed. Several exemplary research studies dealing with experiential learning are reviewed, and the importance of their findings for internship design is highlighted.

A major thrust of experiential learning for adults for a number of years has been to help learners move toward the goal of more self-direction in the learning process. In his doctoral dissertation, Cheren (1978), posited the existence of a "Transitional Dynamic," through which learners, by their own volition and with certain supporting structures, move away from a condition of dependence in learning and toward self-direction. Cheren identified a number of structures and processes that served to facilitate such movement.

Parts Three and Four of this volume, together with a series of forms and worksheets in the Appendix, provide the learner with a model for an internship experience and with tools to implement that model on an individualized or group basis. The model includes pre-assessment, planning, monitoring, and evaluation components that may be used independently or in collaboration with others. Parts Three and Four also contain useful plans and materials for Instructors and Field Supervisors who work with learners in the internship experience. Issues of individual and program evaluation at the formative and summative levels are dealt with specifically. In addition, Part Four presents the results of a research study conducted with participants in an internship experience designed according to a model similar to the one described in this book. Key findings and suggestions for further study are summarized.

Throughout this Guidebook, selections from the literature are included to enrich the reader's understanding of the areas in question and to present differing viewpoints. It has been the authors' intent to provide postsecondary educators who work in field-based learning settings a useful book that combines both theory and guidelines for practice.

## Suggestions for Using the Guidebook

This book is designed so that it may be used in a number of ways, depending upon the needs of the learners, and the needs of the organization. It may be used by individuals, by small clusters of learners in business, social service or other organizations, or by learners enrolled in internship programs at colleges or universities. The model, the procedures, and the worksheets provided, while being used successfully by the authors, may be modified to meet specific requirements, if desired. The addition of individual counseling sessions or group meetings with participants, instructors, and field supervisors beyond those suggested in the text might enrich the learning experience.

It is suggested that instructors and field supervisors confer with the participants regarding specific uses of the various forms and worksheets early in the internship experience. The success of an internship experience depends upon the quality of this three-way relationship.

## Locations for Learning

Traditionally, internships have involved participants at clinical or field locations. Sites have typically been predetermined and systematically assigned, or determined through individual identification and selection. Where large numbers of participants have been involved, placement has been the more common method. Smaller programs, which often involve individual graduate students or other advanced learners, however, usually require that participants take responsibility for selecting a suitable location.

The Guidebook has been designed to serve this broad spectrum of individuals and programs. Even a single, initially unguided learner may effectively use portions of the text to develop and undertake experiential learning activities. Alternatively, groups of participants and instructional personnel will find the text useful in guiding learning while preserving individual planning and experience for each participant.

Before internship sites are assigned or individually selected, it is recommended that instructors and participants confer regarding results of the pre-assessment activities described in the text. Through this process, the learning needs of participants can be more closely matched with the learning opportunities available among potential internship locations.

## Roles of Instructor and Field Supervisor

As envisioned in this Guidebook, the major roles of the instructor and field supervisor are those of facilitators of learning. Each internship participant is expected to assume a good part of the responsibility for learning. In order for this to be done successfully, however, a special kind of climate needs to be created.

One aspect of such a learning climate is respect for the learner as a colleague. While this does not suggest equality in all areas of knowledge

viii

or experience, it does imply an openness to two-way communication regarding ideas and problems. Another characteristic of a facilitative learning climate is support for the learner. Part of the responsibility of the Instructor and the Field Supervisor(s) is to help the participant achieve his or her learning goals. This does not mean to overprotect the learner or to smooth over problems that may arise because of faulty decision-making, but it does mean being available to the participant to discuss problems and suggest resources. A third important part of the learning climate is delegation of authority. Unless the intern is permitted to take on real assignments and to make decisions and live with their consequences, the quality of learning will be mediocre at best. The most productive situations during internship experiences are those where the intern is treated as a professional employee, being expected to contribute to organizational goals and having access to the personnel and material resources of the organization.

It should be the role of the Instructor and Field Supervisor(s) to create and maintain such a climate for learning. In order to do this, frequent communications between them will be extremely helpful. Further information regarding specific activities for the Instructor and Field Supervisor(s) will be found in Parts Three and Four of this volume.

Evaluation and Grading

An evaluation model for the internship experience is presented in Part Four, Chapter 8. The model includes an individual participant evaluation component and a program evaluation component. The Appendix contains several forms that may be used in the formative and summative evaluation processes.

Approaches to the evaluation of the intern include self-evaluation, peer evaluation, instructor evaluation, and field supervisor evaluation. Program evaluation includes assessment of both program design, and effectiveness, and the roles of the Instructor and Field Supervisor(s).

In this volume, great emphasis is placed on formative evaluation - that is, on-going evaluation for the purpose of improvement. One reason for this is related to the point made earlier regarding the facilitative roles of the Instructor and the Field Supervisor(s). It is to everyone's advantage that the Intern have a successful learning experience. Another reason to emphasize formative evaluation is to model effective organizational functioning where learning from experience is a continuing process in the quest for excellence.

However, in the Internship, as in the work world of most organizations, summative evaluation is an essential fact of life. The purpose of summative evaluation is to gather data for decision-making. One decision often required in institutions of higher education is the assignment of a grade to the participant. Another kind of decision that may be made as the result of an internship experience is the decision of whether or where to employ the intern. Decisions regarding the design of future internships may also be made on the basis of summative evaluation data. Such decisions regard modifications which may improve the learning in subsequent offerings of the internship. Whatever the decisions, it is suggested that all participating parties have input into the decision-making process.

Part One

## THE STRUCTURE OF WORK IN POSTSECONDARY ORGANIZATIONS

> Nothing can take the place of practical
> experience out in the world.
>
> - A. B. Zu Tavern

### Introduction

Until recently, the term "postsecondary education" was commonly associated with collegiate institutions serving individuals between the ages of 18 and 22. Such association is limiting because it fails to take into account the broad nature and scope of formal learning opportunities in the adult years.

Whether one is investigating postsecondary education as an inclusive field of study or preparing for a career within one specific sector, it should be understood that postsecondary education (education beyond high school) occurs within many types of institutions and across many sectors of society.

Part One of this text identifies the structure of work in organizations that provide postsecondary education. Chapter 1 enumerates the many types of postsecondary institutions and the scope of their activities as educational organizations. The same chapter also discusses prospects for careers among these alternative educational environments.

Following Chapter 1, a series of selected readings introduces the reader to the specific nature of educator roles among several sectors of postsecondary education. A selection by Jones speaks to traditional career prospects in student affairs among the nation's colleges and universities. The perspective is cautious, but it is cognizant of the significant changes which this sector continues to undergo in response to declining enrollments and changing spending priorities.

Hiemstra, Bashook, McQuigg, and Cristiani and Cristiani present enlightening views of adult education, professional education, and education and counseling in business/industry sectors. The dramatic growth in educational programming among these sectors invites greater participation by those who seek careers in education beyond the elementary or secondary level. Poppenhagen presents recent results of research conducted among non-collegiate postsecondary educators relative to their professional needs and the compatibility of those needs with more traditional graduate preparation programs. Finally, Pinto and Walker provide an overview of practitioner roles in organizations concerned with training and development.

Chapter 1

TYPES OF POSTSECONDARY EDUCATION ORGANIZATIONS:
PERSPECTIVES ON ROLES AND CAREERS

> A school should not be a preparation for life.
> A school should be life.

>                              - Elbert Hubbard

The world of professional education is undergoing a remarkable transformation.  Caught for many years in the assumption that learning occurs mostly between the ages of six and twenty-two, institutions which train teachers have persisted in preparing individuals for roles in schools and, to a more limited degree, colleges and universities.  It is known today, however, that learning, like human development itself, occurs formally and informally throughout life and within diverse settings.

Alvin Toffler (1980), the noted futurist, has speculated that in the future more learning will occur by design outside rather than inside classrooms.  He suggests that the years of compulsory schooling will grow shorter, not longer.  Young and old will mingle as education becomes more interspersed with work and spread out over a lifetime.

Dramatic evidence already exists to support Toffler's predictions.  Table 1 identifies the wide array of education and learning sources which currently attract Americans.  Note particularly that of 63 million adults estimated to be learning within an institutional setting, only 13 million study within colleges and universities.  The vast majority, therefore, participate in both formal and informal learning through job and professional affiliations, voluntary organizations, and social and community agencies.

Harold Hodgkinson (1979) has carefully examined this expanding world of postsecondary education.  His description of its institutional and human aspects is informative:

> The Department of Defense, industry, professional associations, adult education associations, and proprietaries, among others, are the postsecondary "players" with whom you might consider allying yourself.

> Department of Defense.  The Department of Defense would like to have one out of three high school graduates go directly into

Table 1.  Sources of Education and Learning
in the United States*

| Deliberate Education and Learning | Usual Age of Students | Approximate Number of Participants (in millions) |
|---|---|---|
| **I.  Schools** | | |
| A.  Preprimary education | 1-4 | 10.0 |
| B.  Elementary and secondary education | 5-17 | 42.0 |
| C.  College and university undergraduate education | 18-21 | 9.5 |
| D.  Graduate and professional education | 21-27 | 1.5 |
| E.  Public school adult education | 16 and older | 1.8 |
| F.  Proprietary schools | 18 and older | 1.2 |
| G.  University extension and continuing education | 28 and older | 3.3 |
| H.  Community education | All ages | .5 |
| **II.  Nonschool Organizations** | | |
| A.  Private industry | | 5.8 |
| B.  Professional associations | | 5.5 |
| C.  Trade unions | | .6 |
| D.  Government service | | 3.0 |
| **III.  Nonschool Organizations** | | |
| E.  Federal manpower programs | | 1.7 |
| F.  Military services | | 1.5 |
| G.  Agriculture extension | | 12.0 |
| H.  City recreation departments | | 5.0 |
| I.  Community organizations | | 7.4 |
| J.  Churches and synagogues | | 3.3 |
| K.  Free universities | | .2 |
| L.  Parks and forests | | No meaningful estimate |

* Source:  Peterson, R.E.  _Lifelong Learning in America_.  San Francisco: Jossey-Bass, Inc., 1979, p. 15.  Reprinted by permission.


military service.  It would be sporting of them to want the bottom third of the high school class, but no luck -- they want the bright kid and they put a lot of money into advertising.

Industry.  Industry is the ultimate credential.  According to the Conference Board, industry spent $2 billion on in-company education during the past year.  That does not mean money to have their workers go to colleges -- it means programs taught in the industry by people that the industry has hired.  The business term for this is "make or buy" -- you either make it or you buy it.  Four hundred industries have decided to make it instead of buying it. They have, on site, a building called "college," "university," "institute," or "center," and they are teaching enormous numbers of people, right in house. There is a good reason for that: they can control it better, and they think they have a better handle on the outcome if they do it themselves. I believe that $15-20 billion would be an easily documented amount that business is spending on its own system of education. Look at AT&T, for example. They employ 1,000,000 workers and their education budget is $700 million. (For comparative purposes, MIT's is about $220 million.) AT&T employs about 2,000 Ph.D's, mostly in the Bell Labs. (I always thought, "Well, sure, those are the inferior Ph.D's who couldn't get work at Yale, Princeton, or Harvard." The trouble with my theory is demonstrated by the fact that the Nobel prize for physics last year went to two Bell Lab scientists who were working not to develop a new switching device for your telephone but to find the origins of the universe, studying heat signals that come from our galaxy -- and AT&T was paying them to do that.) Indeed, many people decry the lack of basic research going on, but most of it is not in universities anymore. Industry's efforts at providing an educational system are not to be sneezed at.

Professional associations. Then, there are the professional associations which operate their own continuing education programs. In the field of engineering, for example, 86 percent of the professional and technical societies operate such programs, offering 1,100 courses to 30,000 attendees last year.

Proprietaries. There are 9,000 proprietaries in existence, and nobody's worried that they'll go out of business. Indeed, I know the president of a proprietary institution who gave an $8,000 salary increase to one faculty member for being the best teacher on the campus last year. Because these schools are proprietary, they can share profits, and that is exactly what that president was doing. He was saying, "The company did well this year; now you are going to do well." That is a powerful motivator, so the teachers work hard. In addition, they are not concerned with research. They know what they are doing: they are teaching. Research and publication are not for them. As the president of one industry school said, "If our faculty published, we would perish."

Adult education. There is a big growth market in continuing education which, of course, everybody wants to get into. More and more states are passing laws that require a return to college. Since these laws never specify what is to be taught (except in two areas of engineering that I know about), and they do not specify the site, every institution assumes that it will get its share of this new market. There are about eight million people, now, who have to go back to college because of these mandatory, continuing education laws (pp. 10-11).

Career prospects emerge principally from these diverse institutions and organizations in which formal education has become a necessary and an

5

integral activity. Postsecondary educators can look forward to an expanding range of possible uses for their special skills and knowledge.

Of course, appropriate preparation for educational roles in these organizations is essential. Ultimately, it is the organizational environments
more than specific role functions which are likely to vary among postsecondary institutions. Roles once associated only with colleges and
universities are being adopted within business and agency settings as well
as military and health care organizations. Skills once related solely to
collegiate teaching and instructional design now find applications on a
regular basis outside the academy. To be sure, careers continue to be
available and attractive within higher education but individuals interested in postsecondary education need not be restricted to a career in
collegiate settings.

The reading selections which follow were chosen to portray the variety
of postsecondary education careers. Perusal of these readings will reveal
the richness of possibilities for employment in this burgeoning field.

## Selected Readings

STUDENT PERSONNEL WORK: CURRENT
STATE AND FUTURE DIRECTIONS*
John D. Jones

> An overview of recent
> literature, trends, and
> projection on the state
> of the professions.

A great deal has been published
in the past few years regarding
trends in student personnel work
and the future role of the student
personnel administrator. In fact,
one would have to do a considerable amount of reading in order to
keep up with what the current literature is projecting about the
future of the profession.

This article aims to help the
student personnel administrator
who finds that his/her reading time
is being usurped by more pressing
problems. An effort has been made
to locate relevant literature and
to glean opinions regarding the
state of the art and the direction
in which the profession is headed.

The review is organized in such
a manner as to explore (1) the current state of student personnel
work, (2) influences that either
directly or indirectly control the
profession, and (3) changes that

---

*Reprinted with permis-
sion of the publisher
from the NASPA Journal,
Vol. 15, No. 4, 1978,
pp. 2-11.

are presently taking place (i.e.,
role and function changes, organizational structure changes, program trends).

Since World War II the field of
student personnel work has been
in a constant state of transition.
Several trends relating to the
administration of student personnel work were prominent during
these years.

One trend was the "Student Personnel Point of View" which es-
poused the assumption that (a)
students are individuals, therefore individual differences may
be expected, (b) the student
should be treated as a whole person, and (c) all educational
activities start from the developmental stage where the student
is and not the developmental stage
that the institution would prefer
the student to be (Chandler, 1973).
During this period, 10 to 15 different functions (i.e., counseling,
testing, placement, health, extra-
curricular activities, financial
aid, etc.) were identified as the
responsibilities of the student
personnel administrator and the
agencies for delivering services
to students.

A second trend of more recent
vintage involves the terminology
"Student Development." Some have
felt that "Student Development"
is really nothing more than a
synonym for what was previously
called "Student Personnel." However, others contend that "Student
Development" is the application of
human development concepts in
order that students can master
increasingly complex developmental-
al tasks, achieve self direction,
and become independent (Miller
and Prince, 1976). Moreover, the
term implies that the entire institutional setting, as opposed to
specific service agencies, is
responsible for bringing about the
behavioral development of the student.

The Tomorrow's Higher Education Project of the American College Personnel Association is an attempt to reconceptualize student personnel work to emphasize the concept of student development rather than student adjustment. Here, student development is defined as personal development of (1) cultural awareness, (2) value systems, (3) self awareness, (4) interpersonal skills, and (5) community responsibility (Berry, 1976).

In the past decade there has been a movement to establish the role of student personnel as a primary rather than a supportive function in higher education, fully integrated with the academic program. Only limited progress has been made, however, and the battle to achieve full recognition of the student personnel function has not been totally successful (Shoemer, 1977). One of the problems stems from the fact that student personnel work has become almost totally separated from the academic program. This separation has permitted student personnel workers to develop a power base of sorts, but it has also caused the students' education to be split into (1) a required formal curriculum, and (2) an extracurriculum participated in on a voluntary basis (Miller, 1977).

The most recent trend in this transition period is to move student personnel into the academic arena. This is clearly necessary if student development truly is to be an integral part of the institution's mission (Thomas, 1976; Nash, 1977).

TRADITIONAL FUNCTIONS OF STUDENT PERSONNEL

The traditional services and specialized functions provided for students under the student personnel heading have been classified under four general categories by the NASPA Division of Professional Development and Standards (Ruthenberg, 1971).

The first of these is described as "caring functions." Counseling services of various kinds best characterize this work, but a number of other specialized programs, including health services, placement, and financial aid also are included.

The second general category includes those responsibilities that may be identified as "control functions." They begin with recruitment and admissions, since these activities and services determine the general character of the student body and they are closely connected to traditional disciplinary functions. The handling of student behavior problems is a long-standing professional assignment that is now becoming more of a counseling function. Housing, although not usually thought of as related to control, may be included in this category.

The third category of student personnel functions includes the co-curricular and extra-curricular life of the student. These are generally understood to include student political organizations and social and cultural programs.

The fourth general category of these functions, and the most recent of them to become a part of student personnel, are the educational and developmental functions. These include orientation of new students, remedial services, specialized work done with culturally different students, educational programs in residence halls and many other functions that were previously considered to be more closely aligned with the academic sector of higher education.

ROLE AND FUNCTION CHANGES

The new role of the student personnel administrator is characterized by a movement away from the "control functions": a continuation of the "caring functions" and co-curricular functions: and an increased emphasis on the educational and developmental functions.

It is now time for student personnel workers to realize that they have been dealing with only a part of the student. Personal development and academic growth are currently carried on as independent projects. If the student's total development is truly the primary objective, then not only must faculty members become more concerned with student development, student personnel workers must become more actively involved with the academic growth of their students (Miller, 1977). In fact, many authors are advocating erasing the imaginary lines between academic functions and student personnel functions (Harvey, 1974; Brown, 1972; Miller, 1976).

## THE STUDENT DEVELOPMENT EDUCATOR

The term found quite often in the literature that describes the instructional role of the student personnel administrator is student development educator. Student development educators are defined as fully qualified professionals who are able to help students discover the potential of their personal resources and use those resources for continued personal and professional growth (Nash, 1977).

Much of the literature advocating reform in student personnel administration too quickly accepts as inevitable that the future of the student personnel work lies in management or service roles. However, some authors (Nash, et. al., 1975) feel that rather than taking a defensive stand during the period of uncertainty in higher education, student personnel professionals must become student development activists by attaining the training and responsibility needed to become co-equal partners with faculty in the instructional process. Student personnel activists must become advocates for reform in all areas of instruction.

This position regarding role and function change for student personnel workers is supported in the monograph, Student Development in Tomorrow's Higher Education: A Return To The Academy. In this publication, Robert Brown observes the lack of synthesis in the approach to the student's development when faculty and student personnel workers have not been able to successfully join their efforts (Brown, 1972).

In stating his opinion regarding the changing role, Burns Crookston contends that the responsibility of the principal student affairs officer should be milieu management. This refers to the systematic coordination and integration of the total campus environment. Milieu management requires active and persistent direction from the principal student affairs officer, but not the manipulative power of a "big brother." In assuming this position, it must be recognized that the role of higher education has evolved from one of "in loco parentis" to that of producing a product to be consumed. According to Crookston, the primary role of the principal student affairs officer should be to use legitimate power to create an actualizing environment. A key to this theory is that all members of the system be educated in the methods of, and committed to the benefits of community governance (Crookston, 1973).

## A NEW BREED OF STUDENT DEVELOPMENT EXPERTS

In reflecting on Robert Brown's work, Patricia Cross states that she is in agreement with his description of the new role for student personnel workers. Moreover, she sees a new breed of student development experts emerging. These will take on the role of both diagnostician and program technologist. However, the problem, as she presents it, is that at this time not enough is known about student development to produce "experts" or professionals in the field. She predicts that within ten to twenty years, as the result of research and teaching, professional student development experts will evolve (Cross, 1973).

In summarizing the new role of the student personnel administrator, it may be said that this person should be one who does not function primarily as an adversary of the faculty and administration nor as an ally of the student, but rather as an equal partner who seeks to assist all in the attainment of the institution's ultimate goals.

ORGANIZATIONAL STRUCTURE CHANGES

The last few years have seen a recognition of the need for a reorganization of the offices of student personnel administrators as they move more towards the student development approach (Marshall, 1976). However, as Burns Crookston suggests, it may be impossible to move into a model of human development within the bureaucracy that exists in student personnel organizations on most campuses today (Crookston, 1976). As functions and responsibilities change in order to accommodate the "new students," it is only natural that organizational structures must also change.

David Tilley's chapter entitled "Student Services and the Politics of Survival," in the book Services for Students, addresses this subject. Tilley contends that changes in the organization and conduct of student services are required to offset climate of education from expansion and affluence to retrenchment and scarcity (Tilley, 1973).

The conflicting mixture of functions and responsibilities which have been allocated to student personnel services over several stressful decades of expansion have produced what some feel is a weak structure. One of the most practical suggestions for ameliorating this problem calls for two separate branches of student personnel services: student development and student management. The student development branch would be headed by professional student personnel administrators, and the staff would be comprised of professional counselors and student personnel workers. The student management branch would be headed by a person competent in management skills and familiar with legal, business, and safety matters (Prior, 1973). This type of organizational structure would have the advantage of minimizing friction between the control and development aspects of student personnel work. Student rights and responsibilities would be handled by management, which would free student development to concentrate on enrichment programs.

Another viewpoint suggests that the organizational structure for student personnel administration be merged with general educational administration. The purpose of this merger is both to bring student personnel into the mainstream of the university, and to broaden the institution's commitment to the various functions that have previously been delegated to the student personnel division (Harvey, 1974).

Other types of organizational structure changes are prevalent. In most instances the changes are brought about to enhance the student personnel administrator's effectiveness in providing services for students, as well as to enhance communications between the student personnel division and the academic sector of the institution.

CHANGES IN PROGRAM TRENDS

The development of higher education in America has traditionally forced a strict division of the duties and responsibilities that were assigned to academicians and to student personnel administrators. Once divided, the lines have hardened and communications across these lines have become very difficult. Some educators believe that such rigidity seriously interferes with the real work of the institution. It is felt that only through integration of all resources, programs and activities can an institution produce the right education outcomes to educate the whole student and not only his/her intellect (Miller, 1976).

There is evidence of an increase in interest among student personnel administrators in finding new areas of involvement in the academic life of the college or university (Thomas, 1976). Prime areas for the increased involvement by student personnel administrators in academic programming may include the following:

1. Participation by student personnel staff in currently existing academic programs with a joint appointment in an academic department.
2. The expansion of the student personnel counseling functions to include academic advising.
3. Supervision of practicum students and interns from an academic department.
4. The integration of residence hall programs into the academic life of the institution.
5. The assignment of faculty members to residence hall areas to serve as a link between students and the academic sector of the institution.

Following a study of the participation of student personnel administrators in academic programming, Joab Thomas observes that a relatively large proportion of student affairs professionals are engaged in some form of teaching, such as participating in semester-long freshmen seminars in which the personnel advising concept is expanded to include course offerings in academic and vocational guidance. Thomas concludes that the role of the student personnel professional must be expanded to facilitate the academic thrust of the institution (Thomas, 1966).

Chickering suggests several new arrangements for enhancing the effectiveness of commuting students' education. These also have significance for integrating student personnel work with academic programs (Chickering, 1974). The arrangements fall in three major areas and are identified as follows:

1. Student personnel could participate in activities by which students get started, plan their programs, monitor their progress, and make whatever changes are called for as they move along. This would mean involvement by student personnel administrators as well as faculty in admissions, orientation, program planning, and program review.
2. Student personnel administrators and faculty could also collaborate in the areas of teaching, curriculum, and other areas of learning including non-class related field experiences.
3. Short term structured educational experiences planned and implemented jointly by faculty and student personnel workers could serve as an excellent vehicle for involving both groups in the student's total educational process.

Literature related to trends and projections for student personnel administration was reviewed for the purpose of surveying the various authors' opinions. The following conclusions and recommendations are based on a summary of these opinions.

CONCLUSIONS

The profession of student personnel administration has been in a state of transition during the past twenty-five years. Several trends have evolved during this period with the latest being a movement toward more involvement with the academic sector of the college community.

Several factors will apparently influence the direction that student personnel administration will take. As the number of 18 to 22 year olds in college declines and the number of older adult students increases, student personnel programs must be redesigned to accommodate these "new students" who will have different interests and needs.

Other forces within the institution either directly or indirectly will influence student personnel programs. These forces are both driving forces, which involve those that create a positive influence for including the student development concept as an integral part of the academic community; and restraining forces, which impede the integration of the student development concept into the institution's mission. It appears that the weight is more strongly on the side of the driving forces. The movement is toward increased emphasis on student development as a central mission of the institution.

The field is undergoing a role change as several of the traditional functions are no longer viable. The new role of the student personnel administrator is characterized by a movement away from the "control functions," a continuation of the "caring functions" and "co-curricular functions," and an increase on the "educational and developmental functions."

The last few years have seen a recognition of the need for reorganization of the offices of student personnel administrators as they move toward the student development approach. Several models are in various stages of development. An example of one of the most practical organizational structures provides for two separate branches: student development and student management. This type of organizational structure has the advantage of minimizing friction between the control and developmental aspects of student personnel work. Student rights and responsibilities may be handled by student management, thereby freeing student development to concentrate on enrichment programs.

There is evidence of an increase in interest among student personnel administrators in finding new areas of involvement in the academic life of the college or university. A relatively large proportion of student personnel professionals are engaged in some form of teaching, from joint faculty appointments to the supervision of student personnel interns.

At a time when some are advocating retrenchment for student personnel services, the professional student personnel administrator should seize the opportunity to become an instructional expert.

It is time for student personnel workers to recognize that for too long they have been dealing with only a part of the student, and that it is no more valid for them to expect effectiveness in dealing with the student's development independently of his academic life, than it is for the professor to think a student's personal self does not affect his academic growth (Brown, 1972). It is time for all of us to merge both tracks, and share the responsibility for both.

RECOMMENDATIONS

Based on these conclusions and the premise that changes will be necessary to promote the concept of "student development" as one of the primary missions of the institution of higher education, the following recommendations are made:

1.  Student personnel offices and functions must be reorganized to be effective agents for student development. In order to do this, they must move toward a closer relationship with the academic sector and the total college environment, rather than dealing solely with service-oriented ties with students.
2.  College and university presidents should seek ways to involve professional student personnel staff in the academic committee work, implementation of new academic programs, institutional long range planning, etc.
3.  Student personnel administrators should develop competencies in teaching and research, if they do not already possess them. These will provide the opportunity for the student personnel specialist to become co-equal with the faculty.

# REFERENCES

Berry, M. "The state of student affairs: A review of the literature; NASPA Journal, Winter, 1977, 2-3.

Brown, R.D. "Student development and the student personnel worker tomorrow; Some alternative roles", Student Development in Tomorrow's Higher Education - A Return to the Academy. American College Personnel Association Series No. 16, 1972, 37-43.

Chandler, E.M. "Student affairs administration in transition", Journal of College Student Personnel, September, 1973, 14, 392-398.

Chickering, A.W. Commuting Versus Residence Students. San Francisco: Jossey-Bass, 1974.

Crookston, B.B. "Milieu management: An emerging key role of the principal student affairs officer", NASPA Journal, March, 1973, 44-55.

Crookston, B. "Human development - Actualizing people in actualizing organizations", Journal of College Student Personnel, September, 1975, 368-375.

Cross, K.P. "Student personnel work as a profession," Journal of College Student Personnel, 1973, 14, 77-81.

Harvey, T.R. "Some future directions for student personnel administration", Journal of College Student Personnel, July, 1974, 244-246.

Marshall, J.F. and Sorochty, R.W. "Assessing the need to reorganize: A process model", NASPA Journal, Fall, 1976, 13-16.

Miller, T. and Prince, J.S. The Future of Student Affairs. San Francisco: Jossey-Bass, 1976.

Miller, T. "Staff and faculty in-service development: An essential element for student development education", NASPA Region III Review, Fall, 1977, 15-17.

Nash, R., Sauman, K., and Sousa, G. "Student affairs personnel as partners in the instructional venture", NASPA Journal, Fall, 1975, 57-58.

Nash, R.J., Sauman, K., and Sousa, G.M. "Student development educators as teachers and faculty developers: A humanistic view", NASPA Journal, Winter, 1977, 11-25.

Prince, J., et al. "A student development model for student affairs in tomorrow's higher education", Journal of College Student Personnel, July, 1975, 334-341.

Prior, J.J. "The reorganization of student personnel services: Facing reality", Journal of College Student Personnel, 14, 1973, 202-205.

Ruthenberg, D.B. and Gaylord, C. "Student personnel...What is it?" Report of NASPA Division of Professional Development and Standards. Portland, 1971.

Schmidt, M.R. "College student personnel: Two alternatives for the future", Journal of College Student Personnel, September, 1975, 366-367.

Shoemer, J. and Snapp, M.K. "Student personnel as a primary educational function: A battle lost", NASPA Journal, Winter, 1977, 48-51.

Thomas, J. "Academic programming: A new dimension in student affairs", NASPA Journal, Winter, 1976, 66-72.

Tilley, D.C. "Student services and the politics of survival", Services for Students, ed. Joseph Katz, Washington: Jossey-Bass, 1973.

ADULT AND CONTINUING EDUCATION:
ITS PROFESSIONALS*
Roger Heimstra

Who is an Adult and
Continuing Educator?

The question raised by this sectional heading is not an easy one to answer. When one hears the term doctor, lawyer, engineer, school teacher, or bus driver, a fairly stable picture of a role and task comes quickly to mind. However, an adult educator can be thought of as a county agent, a teacher who works with illiterate or foreign-born adults, or often as a "what?"

One of the difficulties in describing a professional adult educator is the fact that so many people are now working with adult learners in different capacities. Consequently, one person who considers himself or herself a professional adult educator might have an entirely different kind of position than another person who is considered an educator of adults.

Many adult education positions throughout the United States are filled with capable people who do not have a formal college degree or who have degrees in other than

---

*Reprinted with permission of the publisher from Roger Heimstra, Lifelong Learning (Lincoln, Nebraska: Professional Educators Publications, 1976)

adult education. In addition, many positions as teachers, counselors, and learning resource center personnel are available to bachelor and masters degree holders in adult education. The point in illustrating the range of positions available in adult education is to show to the interested reader that tremendous opportunities do exist. Thus, anyone who finds satisfaction in working with the adult learner can usually obtain full-time employment doing just that.

Because a variety of opportunities in adult and continuing education is available and because so many people have found special satisfaction in working with the adult learner, a goodly share of people working in the field have arrived there "through the back door." This last phrase is an oft-used one in adult education circles to refer to the many people who find themselves professionally responsible for adult learners without having had any training directly related to adult education.

Such a situation has often meant that additional training and knowledge were acquired through formalized programs or through intensive self-study efforts. Fortunately, as the number enrolled in formal adult education graduate programs and the awareness of adult education opportunities have increased, those professionally trained in adult education have also increased, providing a large corps of people with a good understanding of the adult learner and knowledge of how to develop effective programs for such learners.

The purpose of the next section will be to describe the most common types of roles performed by individuals known as adult and continuing educators. In addition, the particular requisite skills for each type will be included in the discussion.

Types of Adult and
Continuing Educators

There are various types of roles
performed by individuals who consider themselves to be professional
adult educators. The variety of
roles is increasing as the profession matures. However, there appear to be three fairly distinct
categories or types. They will be
described in the following subsec-
tions, with a fourth subsection
added to describe the remaining
mixture of positions.

## Administrative Roles

One very significant role in organizing and implementing adult
education efforts is that of administrator. Whether it be a community
college, a learning resource center,
a YMCA, or a voluntary agency, someone must administer the programs,
be in charge of teacher and student
recruitment, work with the board or
council, develop a suitable budget,
and give the basic program leadership. In addition most state departments of education have one or
more adult education specialists
who administer the state ABE programs and who provide general adult
education leadership to local communities.

Consequently, adult education
administrators must have many of
the same skills as any other type
of program administrator. A problem to be faced, though, is that
adult education is often in a mar-
ginal or supporting role, with
scarce resources, an evolving "ter-
ritory," and an ever-changing cli-
entele base. In addition, the
adult participant is seldom enrolled in educational programs unless
he or she wants to be. This means,
therefore, that the adult education
administrator must thoroughly understand how to involve the adult student in the learning endeavor, how
to design programs based on adult
needs, and how to set up learning
activities that are based on what
is known about how adults learn.
Such an understanding must be the

basis for program planning, for
training teachers, and for coordinating each single effort with a
workable whole.

## Teaching Roles

By far the largest category of
adult educator is that of teacher.
These positions range from full-
time Adult Basic Education teachers to teachers of noncredit evening classes such as knitting, oil
painting, or wills and estate planning, to vocational teachers in a
trade school. However, many adult
education teachers do not earn
their primary incomes in such roles.

Consequently, one of the problems
is how to distinguish between a
teacher who simply has the adult
as student and a teacher who is
trained specifically to facilitate
learning for the adult as student.
Because the field of adult education is in an evolving stage as
compared to most other professions,
probably the largest share of adult
education teachers have had very
little specific training related
to the adult as learner. Hopeful-
ly, as the field matures, as it
gains better financial support,
and as adult teacher-training programs are more fully developed,
this situation can be reversed.

## Professorial Roles

Numerous institutions of higher
education throughout the United
States have either departments of
adult and continuing education or
at least offer classes, primarily
at the graduate level, for prospective adult educators. For
example, in 1973, 21 institutions
of higher education graduated 146
doctoral students in adult and
continuing education.

Those individuals who subse-
quently undertake an adult education professorial role will typically divide their time between
(1) teaching and working with students who are wanting to become

adult educators or to become at least acquainted with the field, (2) carrying out research and scholarly pursuits related to adult education as a profession, and (3) carrying out a variety of service activities that attempt to extend the resources of the department and university beyond the campus walls.

Much of the following section will be related to describing several positions or roles emerging in a variety of agencies. Much of the training and preparation required for people in these roles is carried out by professors and graduate departments of adult education.

Miscellaneous Roles

There are several other recognizable roles that do not fall neatly into any of the above three categories. A rapidly developing area of interest, for example, is that of counselor for adult education students. An adult education counselor will no doubt need many of the other roles described above; in addition, he or she will need to be able to adapt general counseling and testing techniques to adult learners.

Another role somewhat different from the others described to date is that of learning resource center facilitator. Such individuals will need teaching skills, counseling skills, and administrative skills; however, they will also need to be skilled at directing individualized learning, discovering various resources for learning outside the normal classroom setting, and coordinating the learning efforts of several learners progressing at various rates.

Somewhat related to several of the roles already described but still different enough to require explanation is that of the non-traditional "mentor." The recent emergence of and interest in the non-traditional forms of learning

has created the need for faculty leadership somewhat different from what has been typical. Mentors work with learners primarily on a one-to-one basis. Such individuals must serve as teachers, helpers, advisors, and counselors, as well as being a contributor to program-planning effort and a developer of learning resources. Such a person will not only need to thoroughly understand how to work with the adult learner, but also how to discover and coordinate a variety of resources for learning that are available in most communities.

A final professional role to be discussed in this section is one that cannot be described easily by a recognizable title. Consequently, for lack of a better title the term "consultant" will be used. Consultants often serve in program-planning, evaluation, or research positions, frequently on a part-time or short-term basis, and increasingly in federally funded projects. A person in a consultant role might also provide leadership for workshops or conferences, serve as in-service training directors for business and industry, or operate in some politically related capacity. Individuals who serve in these roles often have more specialized expertise such as research, educational psychology, or management skills in addition to general adult education skills.

No doubt several types of positions are not covered in the above classifications. Nor do the descriptions cover the many people working in the adult education field as paraprofessional or volunteer leaders. Such individuals perform a variety of important tasks.

16

PERSPECTIVES ON PROFESSIONS
EDUCATION*
Philip G. Bashook

A Genealogy of Today's
Professions Education:
Where Do You Belong?

A little over 20 years ago a few
people at the medical school in
Buffalo began what has become a
common occurrence in many professional schools:  cooperative efforts between teaching faculty and
professional educators.  Independently of the Buffalo activity, T.
Hale Ham, M.D., who was the archi-
tect of the revolutionary Western
Reserve medical curriculum, established the first Division of Research to medical education in
Cleveland in 1958.  The early efforts spread quickly as some of
the Buffalo leaders moved to other
areas of the United States and
Canada and offered courses and
educational opportunities for
their medical school colleagues.
The most well known and often
modeled was developed by George
Miller, M.D., A Medical Teacher

*Reprinted with permis-
sion of the publisher
from Professions Educa-
tion Researcher, No. 3,
Hulda Grobman, Editor,
St. Louis:  St. Louis
University Medical Cen-
ter, 1979.

Training Program (M.T.T.P.) at
Buffalo and moved, with Dr. Miller,
to Chicago when he set up the Office of Research in Medical Education at the University of Illinois
Medical School in 1959.  Medical
faculty from all over North America
and eventually the world flocked to
learn education at Illinois.  At
about the same time, similar programs with slightly changed emphases were begun at Michigan State
University by Hilliard Jason, M.D.,
Ed.D. in the Office of Medical Education Research and Development,
and Stephen Abrahamson, Ph.D. at
the University of Southern California in the Office of Medical
Education.  Others, some involved
in the Buffalo efforts and some
independently, have developed offices and programs throughout North
America and the world.

These modest beginnings only 20
years ago are the legacy for today's
cooperative efforts by professional
faculty and professionally trained
educators.  I envision them as the
first "generation" of the professions education community.

As the offices headed by Ham,
Miller, Jason, Abrahamson, among
others, attracted educators and
clinicians to their visions for
medical education, more professional educators and clinicians
dedicated their careers to medical
education.  This second generation
is characterized mostly by a pioneering spirit, a diversity of
backgrounds, self-taught principles
of androgeny, and the challenge by
their constituencies to do all
phases of education extremely well
(i.e., teacher training, media
production, curriculum development,
and evaluation).  Speaking with
many of these people today, one is
impressed by the variety of educational endeavors they have pursued,
and for those without medical training, the facility with medical jar-
gon and expertise in health settings.
For the clinically trained medical
educators their educational expertise shines brightly.

The third generation joined these efforts in the late 1960's and early 1970's about the time of increased financial support and recognition to other health professions. Most of these people received advanced degrees in education from the "K-12 oriented" schools of education. A few have backgrounds in higher education and school administration. Two attributes characterize them: a blending of the second generation's generalist approach to medical education with the educational research orientation of their mentors in faculties of education; and their involvement with a variety of health profession areas. However, most seemed attracted to the field because there were opportunities to translate the latest educational theories and concepts in new and relatively uncharted waters.

The fourth generation began in the early 1970's as education generally and health professions education in particular demanded more specialized expertise. These people were attracted to the professions because of a limited job market in the educational community for their unique and sophisticated expertise. Most were characterized by state-of-the-art technical knowledge and skill, a dedication to maintaining this expertise and a feeling that they perceived the health professions as an innovation and experimentation while not yet conditioned to the school system's bureaucracy.

By 1975 many of the original offices of research in medical education and their contemporaries had begun to produce advanced degree graduates with special training in health professions. Graduates of these programs are the fifth generation. Although schools of nursing have been in a similar business for much longer, their educator-type graduates tend to remain in nursing education. The health professions education degree usually weds the traditional conceptions from a faculty of education with concrete examples drawn from the health care setting and opportunities for practical experience. In a sense, this generation represents the first offspring of health professions education.

The present generation has been affected by the tremendous federal financial support for health manpower, the pronouncements about hospital cost containment and over-supply of physicians, public sentiments about health care and demands for accountability in all professions. It is difficult to characterize the present generation, partly because of the federal presence in health professions education today and by lacking a convenient historical perspective. In some ways this sixth generation appears to be an amalgam of generations two and three.

There are a large number of clinicians from all health professions who select education as their specialty either early in their career training or before they establish a final career direction. These people resemble the second generation in many ways except that there are models for rules and opportunities already established in the health community. Another group in this generation resembles the third generation in breadth of educational background that comes prepared with the added experience of consulting on health professions education projects while obtaining their degrees or working as an educator. They seem more aware of the origins of professions education and self-assured about where they might fit.

Finally, there is a newly emerging group which resembles both generations one and three, except for one major difference: they are not in the health professions but in such other professions as law, engineering and business. Those with professional training resemble generation one in their pioneering spirit, their realization that colleagues trained in education could help them and their sense of challenge in addressing educational problems. Those with educational background rather than training in any of these professions resemble generation three except that they have the health professions educators as models and colleagues. They still have roles similar to the earlier generation but limited to their selected professions. The major difference is that they are translating ideas, techniques and models in health professions to other professions rather than from school system education to professions education.

I am not implying that each of these generations stopped with the arrival of the next one, but rather became viable at about the dates cited. Obviously, we can suggest people who fit any of the earlier generations yet are very active today and even may be starting now but resemble an earlier generation.

Where do you belong?

Having suggested these labels, I find it difficult to predict the next generation. Will our growing community be influenced more by the changing federal commitment to health manpower, the challenges to quality legal education, or the oversupply of teachers and faculty for schools of education? Perhaps the influence will be in the research directions linking psychology, sociology, anthropology, education and the professions. Or perhaps, the health professions segment of professions education is THE ESTABLISHMENT which will become staid, starched and an unattractive bureaucracy while the other professions blossom and attract the excited eager newcomers. To paraphrase a famous saying, "I saw the future and it's still under construction."

THE ROLE OF EDUCATION IN INDUSTRY*
Beverly McQuigg

While doubt grows that colleges and universities can or should prepare people directly for the job market, corporations find their education/training role increasingly important. Cooperation between higher education and the corporate world is becoming common.

More and more, education and training are becoming an important part of American business and industry. There is a growing tendency to view one's employees as a resource, and money spent in training and development as an investment rather than an expense. Need, not cost, is the primary factor influencing corporate commitment to training and development. In-house training appears to be exempt from normal managerial decision making, which is heavily cost-oriented.

Most training and development takes place on the job and includes the costs of initial training; retraining each time a job function changes, a new piece of equipment is installed, or a new method or product is introduced; more training each time the employee changes

*Reprinted with permission of the publisher from Phi Delta Kappan, January, 1980, pp. 324-325 ( © 1980, by Phi Delta Kappa, Inc.).

jobs; and replacement training for each new employee.

The peak of interest and activity in training occurs when an organization is growing and is concerned about having an adequate pool of well-trained and educated employees. This is especially pronounced in those organizations committed philosophically (or by union contract) to promotion from within.

Training and development are also important to high-technology corporations. The further toward the "leading edge" the company operates, the more it must educate its own people. It also occurs when an organization's mission or product mix changes and people have to be trained or retrained for new skills and new roles in the new organization.

The need for in-house training and development peaks when the labor market is tight in general or in particular specialties. Academic institutions are seen as having inadequate resources, doing an inadequate job in a specialized area. [1]

Non-business-oriented motives for training - e.g., dedication to the concept of education solely as a means of upgrading a work force - are rare. Corporate motives for training tend to be short-term, functional, and mission-oriented. With only a few exceptions, companies sponsor training and development because they feel they have to - so the work can get done, so that personnel will be ready when needed.

More frequently than ever before, corporate education and training people and their department heads are full-time professionals. Most department heads have direct access to the top executive. The training and development office is becoming increasingly important, providing a career path in its own right. Education staffs are becoming more dispersed. Professionals are more often assigned to field locations.

The primary role of education staffs is program development and administration. Actual teaching is done by the line management - especially the department head - who has the most to say about who is to be exposed to formal training and development activities and to what extent. Line management generally defines training and development needs.

A new study of engineering/scientist continuing education by John Klus and Judy Jones reports that enrollments for in-house continuing education programs are roughly comparable to out-of-plant enrollments. Of the out-of-plant enrollments, it is reported that universities train 114,688, associations train 71,904, and community colleges train 14,000 persons. [2]

A survey by the Bureau of National Affairs among 141 organizations reveals that, for their nonmanagement employees, 55% had formal in-house training; half of these had separate training departments. The types of courses offered by employers ranged from graduate-level work to basic reading and math skills. Ninety percent had tuition aid programs. Employee relations, counseling, and discipline ranked as the most important topics for first-line supervisor training; wage and salary administration and performance appraisal were most important for middle-management training. [3]

Findings from the Bureau of National Affairs concerning management training and developments programs shows that, of 75 large companies (1,000 employees or more) and 39 small companies, 75% had in-house training programs, as opposed to 6% who participated in university development programs. Over half of all the companies also provided training through outside seminars, professional or trade association meetings, and self-training courses. Employers provide training primarily because they feel job skills can best be taught in their own training programs and because they feel that the education and/or training background of their employees is inadequate if they train outside their own programs.[4]

Professional and technical societies are playing an increasing role in meeting the challenge imposed by technological and organizational change, according to a new study by the American Society of Mechanical Engineers. Eighty-six percent of the major professional and technical societies operate or are in the process of developing continuing education programs; 49% cosponsor programs with local universities, and 33% with proprietary organizations. In 1976 these societies offered 1,100 courses to 30,000 attendees.

The Department of Labor's Bureau of Labor Statistics has been studying training by employers in 14 occupations in four metalworking industries. Over 90% of these firms reported that they use the production shop as a training facility. For noncompany facilities, more than 25% reported the use of adult education centers, and more than 10% use community colleges.[5]

A study by Gilbert J. Black shows that American industry invested $1.2 billion in management evaluation and development in 1976. Sixty-two percent of the money went for in-house salaries and administrative costs, while 11% was spent on outside seminars and workshops. The balance, 22%, was divided among consultants, tools and instructional materials, equipment and facilities, tuition refunds, and other expenses. Management development expenditures are expected to be over $2.2 billion in the year 1982.[6]

Dealing specifically with management training and development programs, the Bureau of National Affairs surveyed 75 large companies and 39 small ones in 1977, as I mentioned earlier. It found that for first-level supervisors the most common training activities are on-the-job coaching, tuition

aid for college courses, and in-house training programs. Programs for middle managers involve more outside programs, such as attendance at outside job-related seminars. In-house training programs are provided for first-level supervisors in three-fourths of the companies. More than half the companies have a training and development manager to administer the in-house programs.

The use of outside sources for management training programs is more common in nonbusiness organizations than in business organizations. It is done more frequently in small firms than in large ones, perhaps because small firms are less likely to have experts in certain areas on the payroll. University development programs were attended most by top-level executives for programs of upper-level management.

Large industries have several reasons for doing their training in-house. First of all, such training is often more relevant than training done outside. Knowledge acquired in-house can often be put into practice immediately. The training does not become obsolete before it can be used. Persons in charge of designing the training and development programs are close to the managers of the various divisions within the company and know immediately what the needs are. In-house training is done by using in-house staff who either teach the courses themselves or train the line supervisors to administer the training to persons in their charge. If the training cannot be done by the in-house staff, consultants are hired.

Corporations are designing and teaching courses that will enable employees to earn credit toward undergraduate and master's degrees. Some big corporations and their hometown colleges have had cooperative agreements for years.

Schenectady's Union College, for instance, has given credits toward an advanced degree in power systems engineering for more than 20 years to General Electric Company employees who take G.E.'s courses. In most cases, the students are supervisory workers without college degrees or with only two-year associate degrees. The primary aim of the course is to upgrade their job skills. But if the college credits they receive motivate the employees to embark on further college study, that decision is a splendid fringe benefit for the company, many executives say.

Companies offering college credit courses include Xerox, AT&T, Lockheed Missiles and Space, Holiday Inn, TWA, Bank of America, IBM, and John Hancock Mutual Life Insurance. This is only a sampling, of course. Professional educators analyze each training program before recommending the granting of college credits. Unions, trade groups, and government agencies have also begun to offer their own college credit courses. The American Council of Education conducts detailed evaluations of courses for corporations seeking college credit for their programs. Some state education groups conduct similar assessments. The companies are proud of their accredited courses and want to prove that their in-house courses are "equivalent" to the education provided in the traditional environment of a college campus.

Employees respond positively to accreditation. Students seem to work harder when they know they can earn college credits, says an executive of TWA, and more workers sign up to take company courses once the courses receive college accreditation. Some students feel that the college-accredited company programs are better for them than college courses. The advantage over the typical university course is that many are conducted in just one week of intensive work, so that one becomes totally immersed in the material. Also, because the students are currently employed, instructors can relate the material covered to situations the students are involved in every day.

Four of the largest corporations in America - IBM, Xerox, G.E., and AT&T - now offer bachelor's degrees. The Arthur D. Little firm has received authorization to give an MBA in management. University graduates are dissatisfied and feel they are ill-equipped for the "real world." They want learning of a more practical nature. Colleges and universities must now compete with educational programs offered by industry. Continuing inability of traditional U. S. educational institutions to respond promptly to changing learning needs may explain better than any other factor the expanding role of corporations and profit-making schools in postsecondary education. New technology is squeezing unskilled workers out of the labor market and putting a premium on ever more advanced training. Thousands of displaced workers must adjust to other industries and occupations to earn their livelihood. Who is going to provide the education needed to cope with such change? Traditionally, Americans have relied heavily on formal schools to prepare young people to enter the labor force. This reliance is fading fast. There is a growing public perception that the school system is not keeping abreast, that there is a wide chasm between the courses that schools are offering and the training that people need for the world of work. While educators place a high priority on developing a student's mind and turning out a well-rounded human being, the public seems to be more concerned about jobs.

There is growing doubt that colleges and universities really fulfill this job-market purpose, and there is growing debate as to whether they should.

The university and the corporation have much in common. Certain of their objectives are similar. Each has a responsibility to enhance the quality of life. Even though the two institutions may use different means to bring about this result, they will succeed best if they move forward together, each learning from the other, each making its appropriate contribution. Above all, each must recognize that cooperation, not competition, is in the best interest of the people they serve.

REFERENCES

1. Stanley Peterfreud, "Education in Industry - Today and in the Future," Training and Development Journal, May 1976, p. 36.
2. Robert Craig, National Report for Training and Development (Washington, D.C.; American Society for Training and Development, February 1979), p. 2.
3. Ibid., p. 3.
4. Ibid., p. 8.
5. Ibid., p. 12.
6. Gilbert Black, Report on the Management, Development, and Education Market, 1977-1982 (White Plains, N.Y.: Knowledge Industry Publications, 1977), p. 9.

THE APPLICATION OF COUNSELING SKILLS IN THE BUSINESS AND INDUSTRIAL SETTING*
Therese S. Cristiani
Michael F. Cristiani

To encourage counselors to seek employment in business and industry, the article explores the applicability of their skills within this nontraditional setting and offers suggestions regarding the job search.

Counselors increasingly are recognizing that their skills can be applied in a wide variety of settings. In recent years counseling practitioners have branched into such varied fields as community mental health, consulting, corrections, employment and placement centers, the medical profession, private practice, social and governmental agencies, as well as many other nontraditional settings. Still untapped, however, is counseling services for business and industry. For a profession that has its genesis in the area of vocational education and guidance, it is ironic that so few counselors are actually employed today in business and industry. It is our contention that there

---

is a definite need for counseling applications in business and industry and that counselors can and should market their skills in the business community.

## THE NEED

### New Populations

Why should counselors market their skills in business and industry? One rather obvious reason is that counselors are in need of new populations. Positions in the educational setting, the traditional employment avenue of counselors, have narrowed considerably with the decline in school enrollments and with cutbacks in educational financing. In exploring new populations counselors have typically identified work settings that are already flooded with others in helping professions, notably: psychologists and social workers working in community mental health, in hospitals, in child abuse agencies, and in social service organizations, among others. Because these professionals have a foothold on the market, counselors must begin identifying other populations and work settings in which their background and training are relevant and in which there are jobs. Business and industry meet both of these criteria.

### People-Related Problems in Industry

In fact, it can be demonstrated that business and industry can benefit from the skills counselors have. Here are some reasons. Employees in business and industry experience common emotional and psychological difficulties for which they need counseling services: alcoholism and other drug addiction, marital problems, and psychological conflicts. These personal problems contribute to absenteeism and decreased production and, ultimately, to lowered profits. From an organizational perspective conflicts in interpersonal relationships between managers and subordinates, for example,

affect the production and efficiency of the organization. Thus, a major cost of doing business is people-related. Counselors have the skills to provide both of these direct and indirect services in the business and industrial community.

Why, then, have counselors failed to pursue positions in business and industry? One explanation could be that counselors have a strong identification with, and deep roots in, education. This is frequently accompanied by a negative bias toward business and industry. A second reason might be that there is a deficit of information on how counseling skills could be used productively in the business world. And last, many counselors lack both the information and skills that would enable them to approach the job market effectively. Consequently, it is the purpose of this article to provide information about how counseling skills are applicable in business and industry and to explore various ways to approach the job market in the business and industrial setting. To lay a foundation, a brief historical perspective of the business-related employment of counselors is given.

## HISTORICAL REVIEW

Although an emphasis on productive human relations in business and industry is not a new concept, specified examples of the employment of counselors in this area are not frequently reported in the literature. Sperry and Hess (1976), however, have cited three examples of the employment of counselors in industrial settings. As early as 1914, the Ford Motor Company had a program to advise employees on personal problems and legal matters. Another pioneer in industrial counseling was Macy's Department Store, which has employed a full-time psychiatrist since 1925 to help employees with both personal and work-related concerns. Perhaps the most influential of all industrial counseling programs was that instituted at the Western Electric Hawthorne Plant as a result of the Hawthorne Studies (Dickson & Roethlisberger, 1966). This comprehensive counseling program employed more than 50 counselors between 1936 and 1955. In the 20,000 counseling interviews that were conducted, one third of those interviewed reported problems in their interpersonal relationships. The program instituted at the Western Electric Hawthorne Plant has served as a model for many of the counseling programs established during the 1960s and after.

Today many companies are providing direct counseling services, at least on the corporate level, to help employees with a variety of problems. For example, the Utah Copper Division of Kennecott Copper Corporation established a program in 1969 to provide assistance to alcoholic employees. In 1972 this program, called INSIGHT, was responding to a variety of personal concerns of the company's 32,000 employees and 800 dependents - alcohol, marital, financial, and drug addiction ("Seeking out...", 1972).

As can be noted in the above example, alcoholism ranks among the most prevalent of employee concerns. In fact, the National Institute on Alcohol Abuse and Alcoholism is costing industry $15.6 billion per year in absenteeism and medical care (Mayer & Simons, 1977). Other needs that counseling services are responding to include accidents, absenteeism, career paths, legal matters, marital problems, retirement, relocation, overseas transfers, as well as stress resulting from skills becoming obsolete in a rapidly changing technology. In addition to providing direct counseling services to employees in the above areas, industrial counselors may be asked to advise on corporate policies, educate management about mental health, and aid in the

design of psychologically healthy working conditions. Although the need for counselors in business and industry seems apparent, it is disconcerting that those providing counseling services in this setting are typically psychologists, psychiatrists, and psychiatric social workers, not counselors. Perhaps to become more involved in providing direct counseling services, counselors may have to be more assertive in publicizing their areas of expertise as well as earning more credibility from decision makers in the business community.

INDIRECT SERVICES

## The Training and Development Functions

There is, however, another avenue for counselors who are seeking employment in business and industry. This would involve the area of training managers in basic human relations skills similar to those typically used in the traditional counseling interview. In other words, while the majority of the major companies may not be hiring counselors to provide direct personal counseling services to their employees, they are typically committed to the development of their managers in "people skills." Thus, most of the corporate giants and in fact many of the smaller businesses have "human resource" or "training and development" departments, which, in addition to other training functions, conduct training for their personnel in human relations and other skills. Quite frequently, the training function in people skills is conducted by an outside private counseling firm.

Counselors who are interested in the business setting need to be familiar with the applicability of their skills in training and development because this is an area in which they can become involved and, in fact, to which they have much to contribute. To demonstrate this, the applicability of traditional counseling skills to the training of managers will be explored here before the more practical considerations of how to approach the job search are discussed.

Regardless of their specific responsibilities, experts say that managers spend a great deal of their time in interactions on the job with subordinates, peers, or superiors. How they manage others and effectively use their time with others will dictate whether the human resources of a company are being employed to their fullest potential to achieve business results. However, managers are often promoted to management positions because of technical skills and abilities, not necessarily because they have competent interpersonal skills (Sperry & Hess, 1976). In fact, once they become managers their inability to deal effectively with others often costs them further promotions. Many managers are often denied promotions because of their lack of people-related skills, and although they may excel initially, they probably will not make it to the upper levels of management (Levinson, 1978). Is it any wonder then that the top decision makers are alloting more funds for upgrading the people-related skills of their managers? In the area of management development alone, American corporations currently are spending an estimated $1 billion or more a year (Murray, 1979). How, then, are traditional counseling skills being used in training and development programs for managers?

## Management Training

As discussed above, the interpersonal process of communication is an integral component of successful management, just as it is a counseling relationship. Therefore, one way to improve the superior-subordinate relationship is to train managers in some of the more effective counseling skills that improve interpersonal relationships and build trust and rapport with subordinates (Frunzi & Dunn, 1974). These basic counseling skills might include, for example: (a) open-ended leads, (b) summary statements; and (c) empathic responses.

## Counseling Skills for Managers

Let's take a look at how such skills can be applied to management. A skill such as open-ended leads allows the managers to conduct open conversations with their subordinates, and rather than assuming an authoritarian stance in decision making, they learn to encourage subordinate input in the decision-making process. Once managers learn to initiate conversations, other skills, such as summary statements and empathic responses, help the managers practice listening to opposing views and accepting subordinate opinions without prejudgment. Managers find that candor frequently develops between themselves and their subordinates when differing viewpoints can be aired without recrimination. An important effect of using empathic responses in the superior-subordinate relationship is that managers who have been uncomfortable dealing with emotions become more skillful in dealing with the feelings of their subordinates, especially those of a hostile nature. In fact, the manager's ability to reflect back to the subordinate the strong feelings that are being expressed communicates to the subordinate that the manager understands and is willing to listen. This skill can make the difference in a manager's success or failure (Whitehead, 1978). Training programs may not teach the various levels of empathic responses or even label them as such, but managers can be taught to recognize emotions and to deal with them in a constructive fashion. Managers trained in these skills have found that having alternatives for dealing with emotions is an effective management tool in helping to resolve conflicts.

Other parallels can be drawn between the counseling relationship and the superior-subordinate relationship. One such parallel is a process known in the business world as "coaching and counseling." In coaching and counseling, the manager guides, directs, and "coaches" the subordinate on an ad hoc basis concerning job tasks and skills. Additionally, the manager discusses, clarifies, or "counsels" the subordinate in dealing with others or in meeting behavioral objectives in the work setting. The result is increased subordinate development and on-the-job effectiveness (Buzzotta, Lefton & Sherberg, 1977).

Managers can also use their interpersonal skills in performance appraisals that are also formal evaluation reviews. In these reviews it is important for the manager to increase subordinate involvement, understanding, and commitment to job tasks and to organizational goals. By getting the subordinates' inputs there is an increased probability that the subordinates will accept responsibility and develop insight into their impact on performance objectives. When the supervisor properly applies communication and motivational skills in a performance appraisal, the superior also learns about the subordinate's self awareness, commitment and drive, and ability to self-manage, all of which are important factors to be considered in assigning tasks and in determining promotions as well as terminations. In addition, if managers can help subordinates to become more effective, the managers can spend their energies in a proactive rather than a reactive mode.

These and other skills can and are being taught in business through a variety of programs, many of which incorporate the methodologies employed but not exclusive to those used in counselor education. For example, these training programs frequently maximize their impact by incorporating group dynamic principles,

team building, inter- and intra-group processes, and structured group experiences as part of the learning process. Coupled with adaptations of such counselor training methodologies as interpersonal process recall (Kagan, Krathwohl, & Farquhar, 1965) and microcounseling (Ivey, 1971), some management development programs are using audio and video tape playback, critiquing managerial behavior, and teaching managers how to give as well as receive constructive and growth-producing feedback. Behavior rehearsal, modeling tapes, and other educational devices can be incorporated into training programs in which basic objectives include skill building, behavior change, as well as personal insight and increased awareness of one's impact on others.

APPROACHING THE JOB MARKET

From this discussion it is clear that traditional counseling skills are useful to managers in business and industry and that these skills form the basis for many training programs that are conducted for managers and sales personnel. Because this is so, it follows that people with specific training in these skills would have much to offer companies that are committed to training and development. The problem most counselors confront is how to approach this particular job market for employment. The issue is a complicated one because the organizational structure varies tremendously from company to company. To help counselors approach this job market, we will review some guidelines regarding the structure and responsibilities of various departments that typically perform the training and development function, and offer a few suggestions on how to tackle the job search in this area.

Personnel Departments

Frequently, counselors interested in employment in business and industry begin their job search with the personnel department, assuming that it is in this department that they might locate a position in the interpersonal relations field. Personnel departments, however, are typically involved with other responsibilities such as health, safety, salaries, vacations, compensation, sick leave, insurance, housing, recruitment, and personnel records. Thus, personnel departments are not necessarily the place to begin a job search, especially because secretaries and others in these departments are usually instructed to discourage job applicants by telling them there are no available positions.

Training and Development Departments

Many job seekers are unaware that most companies do have, in addition to their personnel departments, and in some instances as a branch of it, a department in which the primary function is training and development. This department is typically labeled one of the following: training and development, education, human resources development, or industrial relations. While the responsibilities of these departments will vary to meet the particular needs of the organization, quite frequently a major component of their training function will be in the area of human relations skills for personnel. Other departmental functions may include areas in which a traditional counseling background is highly advantageous. For example, counseling skills are easily applicable to such topics as time management, conflict resolution, assertiveness training, affirmative action, group skills, problem solving (analysis and prevention), career planning, employee relations, and performance appraisal skills.

Some Suggestions

From the above brief description of the training and development function in business and industry it is apparent that counselors could become a vital part of many business and industrial organiza-

tions. The problem seems to be one of lack of information and resources. Should this be the case, here are a few additional suggestions to those with counseling backgrounds for approaching jobs in the industrial or business setting.

1. Become familiar with the American Society for Training and Development (ASTD); read the ASTD Journal and attend meetings of local chapters. This is an excellent way to meet those people who have interests similar to yours and who are working in the field. They may be able to give you specific suggestions about approaching the job market in your location, possibly providing leads and contacts in your area.

2. Conduct library research in the area of training and development; become familiar with readings by major business authors.

3. Take business courses in industrial psychology and management. Strengthen your background in the behavioral sciences if needed.

4. Do not be intimidated by employers who try to discourage you because of your lack of experience in the business world. You have the essential skills and expertise that are part of training and development in the business community. The first person to convince is yourself!

CONCLUSION

Counselors must begin to search for applications of their skills in non-traditional settings if they are to survive. It has been our purpose to inform counselors regarding the applicability of their skills in business and industry. Not only will the business and industrial community benefit from direct and indirect counseling services, but quite pragmatically, this population has the financial resources to hire counselors. We are convinced that, given some basic information regarding the job search, counselors can not only find employment but can also make a significant contribution to the business community.

## REFERENCES

Buzzoita, V.A.; Lefton, R.E.; & Sherberg, M. Coaching and counseling: How you can improve on the way it's done. Training and Development Journal, 1977, 31 (11), 50-60.

Dickson, W.J., & Roethlisberger, R.J. Counseling in an organization: A sequel to the Hawthorne Researches. Boston: Division of Research, Harvard Business School, 1966.

Frunzi, G.L., & Dunn, J.R. Counseling subordinates: It's up to you. Supervisory Management, August 1974, pp. 2-9.

Ivey, A.E. Microcounseling Innovations in interviewing training. Springfield, Ill.: Charles C. Thomas, 1971.

Kagan, N.; Krathwohl, D.; & Farquhar, W. International process recall: Stimulated recall by videotape. Educational Research Series, No. 24, East Lansing, Michigan State University, 1965.

Levinson, H. The abrasive personality. Harvard Business Review, 1978, 56 (3), 86-94.

Mayer, A., & Simons, P. Management: Company shrink. Newsweek, 24 October 1977, p. 96.

Murray, T.J. What price management education? Dun's Review, March 1979, pp. 104-106.

Seeking out employees' problems. Management Review, April 1972, pp. 38-39.

Sperry, L., & Hess, L. When Charlie's problem becomes your problem: A "contract counseling"

case study. Training and Development Journal, 1976, 30 (2), 54-59.

Whitehead, R. Emotion can make or break a manager. Industry Week, 1978, 196 (5), 73-77.

TRAINING AND DEVELOPMENT
PRACTITIONER ROLES*
Patrick R. Pinto
James W. Walker

1. Needs Analysis and Diagnosis
   - Construct questionnaires and conduct interviews for needs analysis, evaluate feedback, etc.

2. Determine Appropriate Training Approach
   - Evaluate the alternatives of "ready-made" courses or materials, use of programmed instruction, videotape, computer managed and other structured techniques versus a more process-oriented organization development/team-building approach.

3. Program Design and Development
   - Design program content and structure, apply learning theory, establish objectives, evaluate and select instructional methods.

4. Develop Material Resources (Make)
   - Prepare scripts, slides, manuals, artwork, copy, programmed learning, and other

---

*Reproduced by special permission from the July 1978 TRAINING AND DEVELOPMENT JOURNAL. Copyright 1978 by the American Society for Training and Development, Inc.

instructional materials.

5. Manage Internal Resources (Borrow)
   - Obtain and evaluate internal instructors/program resource persons, train others how to train, supervise their work.

6. Manage External Resources (Buy)
   - Hire, supervise, and evaluate external instructors/program resource persons, obtain and evaluate outside consultants and vendors.

7. Individual Development Planning and Counseling
   - Counsel with individuals regarding career development needs and plans; arrange for and maintain records of participation in programs, administer tuition reimbursement, maintain training resource library, keep abreast of EEO.

8. Job/Performance-Related Training
   - Assist managers and others in on-the-job training and development: analyze job skill and knowledge requirements, determine performance problems.

9. Conduct Classroom Training
   - Conduct programs, operate audio-visual equipment, lecture, lead discussions, revise materials based on feedback, arrange program logistics.

10. Group and Organization Development
    - Apply techniques such as team-building, intergroup meetings, behavior modeling, role-playing, stimulation, laboratory education, discussions, cases,

issues.

11. Training Research
    - Present and interpret sta-
      tistics and data relating
      to training; communicate
      through reports, proposals,
      speeches and articles:
      design data collection.

12. Manage Working Relationships
    with Managers and Clients
    - Establish and maintain
      good relations with man-
      agers as clients, counsel
      with them and explain
      recommendations for train-
      ing and development.

13. Manage the Training and De-
    velopment Functions
    - Prepare budgets, organize,
      staff, make formal pre-
      sentations of plans,
      maintain information on
      costs, supervise the work
      of others, project future
      needs, etc.

14. Professional Self Development
    - Attend seminars/conferences,
      and keep abreast of train-
      ing and development con-
      cepts, theories, and tech-
      niques; keep abreast of
      activities in other organ-
      izations.

PREPARING EDUCATORS FOR TRAINING
AND DEVELOPMENT: COMPETENCIES
FOR PERFORMANCE AND MARKETS
FOR EMPLOYMENT

Brent W. Poppenhagen*

Traditionally, colleges of education have concentrated almost exclusively on elementary and secondary teacher preparation or attendant specialities such as school administration. More recently, student and community interests have combined to suggest a broadening of program emphasis to also serve business and health care facilities, government training programs, and other non-profit agencies, such as museums, private welfare institutions, and professional societies wherever educators are needed.

Following this broader emphasis, programs in postsecondary education could emerge at either graduate or undergraduate levels. Postsecondary education would then be viewed as education beyond high school, serving two and four year colleges and universities, institutes, proprietary schools, business and industry training programs, and educational agencies that serve adult populations in any setting.

With appropriate market and skills assessment information, collegiate

*The author was coordinator of the Graduate Program in Higher Education at Cleveland State University, Cleveland, Ohio 44115, when this study was undertaken.

program planners can review staff availability as well as other institutional resources and initiate processes for planning and delivering programs in postsecondary education. Goals related to program development might include but not be limited to:

1. Making the collegiate institution responsive to the needs of previously unserved but prospective students.
2. Serving the growing community of adult educators by identifying their needs and delivering a program to meet those needs.
3. Demonstrating the potential for program flexibility in preservice or graduate education degree programs.

Related Inquiry

A review of research related literature and working documents relative to the competencies of trainers in noncollegiate settings served as a beginning point for the study. Among these are documents developed by the Public Service Commission of Canada (2, 12, 13) and the U.S. Civil Service Commission (14). They identify broad areas of competency related to instructional and consulting skills required by training and development personnel in public service agencies. An illustrative list of these skills includes, but is not limited to, skills in communication, course design, program evaluation, training materials and equipment, and needs analysis. Other items on the Public Service Commission lists, less known even to higher and adult education specialists, include the use of business literature, organizational development theory and manpower planning.

Briers (1) has identified six important capabilities required of industrial technologists: literature of business, management, development, organizational structure, business as an institution, group and personal dynamics, and training issues. The similarity of items from the public service agency documents and the Briers list, to competencies or objectives common to professional education programs is instructive.

Also of interest were the means by which training and development specialists gain knowledge and skills. Here the literature of adult education was instructive. Space will not permit review of the vast literature concerned with adult learning; however, an examination of literature related to Knowles' (4, 5, 6) assumptions and processes of pedagogy and andragogy served as a beginning point. The research of Kolb (7) and Kolb and Plovnick (8) in the development of learning style inventories related to professional career development were also helpful. Working documents such as the Methods Identifier for Gaining Knowledge, Skill and Attitudes (9) were particularly helpful since they are in use in corporate settings.

Purpose of the Assessment

This study was undertaken to: (a) Assess the interest for baccalaureate and master's level training and development specialists among business, health, government and non-profit organizations; (b) Assess the interest in continuing education for training and development specialists: (c) Specify the competencies needed by training and development specialists; (d) Identify the competencies training and development personnel thought were most essential to a postsecondary education program; and (e) Identify the background, prior training, and associated personnel characteristics of incumbent training and development specialists.

Methodology of Assessment

To accomplish the purposes of assessment, a mail survey technique was chosen, using a specifically designed questionnaire instrument. This process provided data which were analyzed using descriptive statistical measures and the chi-square test for significance of difference between variables (10).

Population: For the purpose of this needs assessment, the survey population was identified as the membership of the American Society for Training and Development (ASTD) of Northeast Ohio. This region includes members from Cuyahoga and four surrounding counties. ASTD membership was deemed appropriate as the Association welcomes and enrolls persons from a variety of settings, including businesses, health care institutions, and community agencies of many types.

ASTD membership rolls listed 250 persons at the time of survey distribution. Of these members, approximately 100 were reported by ASTD officers as active in society affairs and therefore likely to participate in the survey. A response of 75-100 was, therefore, deemed adequate for purposes of this research.

The active ASTD membership comprised an estimated 10 percent of the Northeast Ohio human resources development personnel whose roles make them potential clients of professional education programs.

Instrumentation: A three-part survey questionnaire was designed for the study (11). Part I consisted of ten questions, each constructed to yield data about the nature of training and development in the respondent's work setting. Items for this section were devised following suggestions from eight adult and higher education specialists, a panel of six training and development specialists, and an adult education consultant.

Part II consisted of a grid listing 23 "areas of competency." Respondents were asked to check off the competencies which they considered appropriate for a training and development person working as an Instructor, Designer, Manager, Consultant, or Counselor. Area of competency items were suggested by public service agency training and development competency lists (1, 2, 12, 13, 14). Selected items were modified or augmented using objectives from an existing professional preparation program (3).

Part III of the questionnaire asked the respondents to contribute information regarding personal experience and background in the field of training and development.  The questionnaire items were designed following expert consultation as with Parts I and II.

The questionnaire was revised following a review of items and forms by two recognized experts in post-secondary and adult education and the panel of training and development specialists identified earlier.  The questionnaire was next administered to a group of eight training and development specialists.  Final adjustments were then made in format and individual item content.  The questionnaires were mailed to the assessment population during January, 1979.

Analysis and Findings

Of the 100 Postsecondary Education Questionnaires (PEQ), 81 were returned in a form usable for analysis.  Among the 80 respondents were 48 males and 32 females.  Table 1 identifies the majority of subjects (56 percent) as holding a bachelor's degree.  Twenty-eight percent held the master's degree, while 10 percent of the subjects reported holding a doctorate.  Table 1 also reports the respondents' diverse job titles and background prior to entering the training and development field.

Market needs:  Table 2 lists the items and summary statistics of responses pertaining to the market needs for training and development specialists.

The vast majority of subjects (94 percent) identified their organizations as employers of training and development personnel.  Forty-eight percent reported employment of some non-degreed persons.  Sixty-three percent reported employment of some persons who held a bachelor's degree.  Forty-five percent reported employment of some master's degree personnel, while 24 percent of the subjects indicated that their organization employed training and development persons who in some cases held doctoral degrees.  The data identifies a standard for employment which includes advanced education.

Over 60 percent of the subjects reported a need which existed for personnel with either the bachelor's or master's degree.  What is more, 93 percent of the subjects reported a need for courses not necessarily leading to a degree.  It would appear that an impetus exists not only for degree achievement but also for course work applied to inservice education objectives.

Data from item 8 of Table 2 provide additional insight to this identified need for advanced preparation.  The assessment subjects were asked to describe training and development personnel in their organization by selecting appropriate descriptors from among 11 possibilities.  The four most frequent responses included:  persons whose careers are young, persons who have held several positions in the organization, persons moving to leadership positions and former school educators.  These responses identify training and development persons whose need for further education might be viewed as immediate.  For example, persons whose careers are young have had little opportunity to develop competencies solely through experience and may, therefore, benefit from advanced educational programming.  Persons who have held several positions in an organization may require immediate training to facilitate their current role before moving on to still other organizational roles.  Even former school educators, having been formally trained as instructors, may require continued education to master new competencies.  Only 20 percent of the subjects described any of their organization's training and development personnel as having no previous knowledge of training and development as a professional activity.

A case in favor of degree program development was established by the reported need for bachelor's and master's level specialists and by the data reporting characteristics of current training and development personnel.

However, the case in favor of degree program development can be no stronger than the market for grad-

TABLE 1

TRAINING AND DEVELOPMENT SPECIALISTS' BACKGROUND

BY JOB TITLE, EDUCATION, AND PRIOR OCCUPATIONS

| Item | Response | % | N(81) |
|------|----------|---|-------|
| Current job title | Training Manager | 32 | (26) |
| | Training & Development Manager | 4 | (3) |
| | Staff Development/Human Resources Manager | 16 | (13) |
| | Director of Education | 11 | (9) |
| | Organizational Development Manager | 4 | (3) |
| | Asst. Administrator Hospital Educ. | 7 | (6) |
| | Financial Specialist | 3 | (2) |
| | Executive Director | 3 | (2) |
| | Program Director | 1 | (1) |
| | Not responding | 16 | (20) |
| How field of T&D was entered | Choice | 4 | (3) |
| | Promotion | 15 | (12) |
| | Transfer | 3 | (2) |
| | Organizational Need | 8 | (7) |
| | Military | 4 | (3) |
| | Nursing | 10 | (8) |
| | Teaching | 11 | (9) |
| | Personnel | 4 | (3) |
| | Sales | 1 | (1) |
| | Communications | 8 | (7) |
| | Not responding | 32 | (20) |
| Subject's highest education | Non-Degree | 6 | (5) |
| | Bachelor | 32 | (26) |
| | Bachelor + | 24 | (19) |
| | Master | 17 | (13) |
| | Master + | 11 | (9) |
| | Doctorate | 8 | (7) |
| | Doctorate + | 1 | (1) |
| | Not responding | 1 | (1) |

Note:  Number of respondents (N) in parenthesis.

TABLE 2

MARKET NEEDS FOR TRAINING AND DEVELOPMENT SPECIALISTS

| | Question | Percent Responding* | Mean% |
|---|---|---|---|
| 1. | Does organization employ T&D personnel? | | |
| | Yes | 94 | |
| | No | 6 | |
| | If yes, degree held | | |
| | None | | 48 |
| | Bachelor | | 63 |
| | Masters | | 45 |
| | Doctorate | | 24 |
| 2. | Need for bachelors T&D personnel | | |
| | Yes | 67 | |
| | No | 33 | |
| 3. | Need for graduate T&D personnel | | |
| | Yes | 62 | |
| | No | 37 | |
| 4. | Need of T&D for non-degree courses | | |
| | Yes | 93 | |
| | No | 5 | |
| 5. | Financial support to T&D personnel | | |
| | Yes | 92 | |
| | No | 8 | |
| 6. | Job market for T&D personnel | | |
| | Excellent | 7 | |
| | Good | 26 | |
| | Fair | 38 | |
| | Poor | 30 | |
| 7. | Turnover of T&D personnel | | |
| | Rapid | 4 | |
| | Occasional | 46 | |
| | Stable | 50 | |
| 8. | Description of T&D personnel** | | |
| | Careers are young | | 56 |
| | Held several positions in organization | | 51 |
| | Moving to leadership position | | 49 |
| | Former school educators | | 41 |
| | Careers established | | 38 |
| | Moved laterally | | 35 |
| | Business persons with O.D. background | | 31 |
| | Trained O.D.'s | | 28 |
| | Little previous knowledge of O.D. or business | | 20 |
| | Other | | 12 |

\*    N = 80
\*\*    Note: Descriptors ranked from high to low by frequency of occurence.

uates. Items 6 and 7 of Table 2 illuminate the question of potential employment. Sixty-four percent of the subjects indicated that the job market for training and development personnel was fair to good, meaning that occasional openings occurred, while 32 percent responded that the market was good to excellent, meaning that openings occurred frequently. This data was somewhat surprising at a time of economic uncertainty, projected recession, and the heavily reported migration of business and industry from Northern areas to Southern "sunbelt" regions. Fifty percent of the respondents identified occasional turnover among their training and development personnel, while the remaining subjects identified their staffs as stable. The mean number of projected training and development position openings for 1979 was 1.9. The range of reported position openings was 1 to 9, suggesting again that the turnover of personnel is not frantic but that opportunities certainly occur.

Ninety-two percent of the respondents reported that their organization provided financial support to the continuing education of training and development staff. Types of support included tuition reimbursement, released time, paid internships, leaves of absence, salary increase, travel and seminar expense.

Table 3 illustrates selected PEQ items which were analyzed by comparing four organizational groups: (a) Health care institutions (HLT), (b) Government agencies (GOV), (c) Non-profit agencies (NPR), and (d) Business (BUS). Chi-square tests were computed for the data illustrated in Table 3 to determine whether the four groups differed significantly from a random distribution of occurrences (p < .05). No significant difference was found among the four organizational groups. However, several differences among organizational types do warrant discussion. One hundred percent of subjects representing health care institutions, 86 percent representing government agencies, and 98 percent representing business enterprises indicated that their organization employs training and

development personnel. Of the subjects responding from non-profit organizations, only 57 percent reported employing training and development specialists which may reflect limiting financial conditions among such agencies.

Results were similar for items dealing with the need for bachelor's, master's and non-degree courses of study. Subjects representing health and government sectors identified a need for bachelor's level personnel in 82 percent and 86 percent of their responses. Sixty percent of the business sector respondents indicated a similar need while less than 50 percent of the non-profit sector respondents concurred. Findings vary slightly when considering the need for master's level personnel. Again, government (67 percent) and health (76 percent) sectors lead in asserting a need for personnel holding a graduate degree. Seventy-six percent of respondents from health care organizations asserted the need for master's level specialists. A higher percentage of subjects from non-profit organizations (57 percent) expressed the need for graduate degree personnel than did business sector respondents (55 percent).

All four organizational types were reported to need courses not necessarily leading to a degree. Ninety-six percent of business and health sector respondents identified this need, while 86 percent of government and 67 percent of non-profit respondents agreed.

When distributed across the four organizational types, the characteristics of current training and development personnel remain constant for health, government and business organizations. Identified most often as characteristic were persons with young careers, those moving to leadership positions, persons with school education backgrounds and those who had held more than one position in an organization. Subjects from the non-profit sector most often identified persons moving to leadership positions and former school educators as characteristic.

## TABLE 3

### MARKET NEEDS FOR TRAINING AND DEVELOPMENT SPECIALISTS AMONG
### HEALTH, GOVERNMENT, NON-PROFIT AND BUSINESS ORGANIZATIONS

| | HLT | (22) | GOV | (7) | NPR | (7) | BUS | (45) |
|---|---|---|---|---|---|---|---|---|
| **1. Do you employ T&D personnel?** | | | | | | | | |
| Yes | 100% | (22) | 86% | (6) | 57% | (4) | 98% | (44) |
| No | 0% | | 14% | (1) | 43% | (3) | 2% | (1) |
| **2. Need for bachelor degree T&D personnel?** | | | | | | | | |
| Yes | 82% | (18) | 86% | (6) | 43% | (3) | 60% | (25) |
| No | 14% | (3) | 14% | (1) | 57% | (4) | 40% | (17) |
| **3. Need for graduate degree T&D personnel?** | | | | | | | | |
| Yes | 76% | (16) | 67% | (4) | 57% | (4) | 55% | (22) |
| No | 19% | (4) | 33% | (2) | 43% | (3) | 45% | (18) |
| **4. Need for non-degree T&D personnel?** | | | | | | | | |
| Yes | 100% | (22) | 86% | (6) | 67% | (4) | 96% | (42) |
| No | 0% | | 0% | | 33% | (2) | 4% | (2) |
| **5. Financial support available?** | | | | | | | | |
| Yes | 100% | (23) | 71% | (5) | 57% | (4) | 96% | (43) |
| No | 0% | | 29% | (2) | 43% | (3) | 4% | (2) |
| **6. Job market for T&D personnel.** | | | | | | | | |
| Excellent | 5% | (1) | 0% | | 0% | | 9% | (4) |
| Good | 27% | (6) | 14% | (1) | 20% | (1) | 28% | (12) |
| Fair | 36% | (8) | 57% | (4) | 20% | (1) | 37% | (16) |
| Poor | 32% | (7) | 29% | (2) | 60% | (13) | 26% | (11) |
| **7. Turnover of T&D personnel.** | | | | | | | | |
| Rapid | 5% | (1) | 0% | | 0% | | 5% | (2) |
| Occasional | 36% | (8) | 67% | (4) | 40% | (2) | 49% | (21) |
| Stable | 59% | (13) | 33% | (2) | 60% | (3) | 46% | (20) |

Number (N) in parenthesis.

More than 68 percent of the subjects from health, government and business sectors indicated that the job market for training and development personnel was fair to excellent. Only in the case of non-profit organizations were the job prospects seen by more than 50 percent of the respondents as poor. Fifty-nine percent of the health and 60 percent of the non-profit organization respondents identified the turnover of training and development personnel in their organizations as stable. However, 53 percent of business and 67 percent of government respondents characterized the turnover of personnel as occasional or even rapid.

All four organizational types provide financial assistance for continued education. Evidence of this support is strongest in the health care and business sectors. One hundred percent of health care respondents and 96 percent of business respondents indicated that financial support was available from the organization. Seventy-one percent of the respondents from business and 57 percent from the non-profit sector indicated similar support.

Educational competencies needed by training and development specialists: Consultation with persons working in the field of training and development suggested that a high degree of compatibility was likely between the skill needs of training and development specialists and the traditional content of educator preparation programs.

The needs assessment served in testing this informal hypothesis by listing 23 areas of competency (Table 4) which respondents rank ordered as to importance for each of five categories of specialists, i.e. Instructor, Designer, Manager, Consultant and Counselor.

For purposes of this discussion, the five categories of training and development personnel will be viewed in light of those competencies to which respondents assigned top priority. Ranked as priorities for Instructors were competencies pertaining to training equipment and materials handling,

communication skills, human relations skills, teaching practice, knowledge of learning theory, and knowledge of adult psychology. Most important for Designers were course design skills, knowledge of learning theory, research methods, knowledge of training equipment and materials, communication skills, program evaluation skills, and training needs analysis skills. Managers were identified as requiring administrative skills, manpower planning skills, human relations skills, and team building skills. Consultants were recognized as needing communication skills, team building skills, knowledge of adult psychology, group dynamics, knowledge of organizational characteristics, human relation skills, and knowledge of the literature of business/education. Finally, persons filling counseling roles were seen as requiring knowledge of adult psychology, human relations, communication skills, social issues, group dynamics, and diagnostic skills.

Common among the top six competencies for each category of training and development specialist was communication skill. Recognized under four categories was human relations skill while knowledge of adult psychology and development was placed among the top six for each of three categories.

Subjects from health, government, non-profit, and business sectors, maintained nearly identical perceptions of the competency requirements for each training and development personnel category. It is likely that the various roles played by training and development specialists are not so discrete as this study's five groups of specialists would suggest. More likely is the idea that training and development specialists perform more than one role and perhaps all five under varying circumstances, thereby using competencies from each of the five categories.

It appeared then that congruence between training and development as a professional education activity and traditional education programs

# TABLE 4

## ESSENTIAL COMPETENCIES FOR TRAINING AND DEVELOPMENT EDUCATORS

| | CATEGORY OF TRAINING AND DEVELOPMENT PERSON | | | | | | | | | |
|---|---|---|---|---|---|---|---|---|---|---|
| AREAS OF COMPETENCY | Instructor | | Designer | | Manager | | Consultant | | Counselor | |
| | Rank | % | Rank | % | Rank | % | Rank | % | Rank | % |
| 1. Administration skills | 18 | 34 | 17 | 28 | 1* | 84 | 14 | 46 | 14 | 24 |
| 2. Knowledge of social issues | 12 | 49 | 13 | 45 | 11 | 61 | 6 | 63 | 3* | 62 |
| 3. Research methods and applications | 17 | 35 | 3* | 70 | 15 | 49 | 5 | 65 | 15 | 21 |
| 4. Communication skills | 2* | 84 | 4* | 67 | 3* | 79 | 1* | 73 | 2* | 69 |
| 5. Course design skills | 9 | 56 | 1* | 78 | 18 | 24 | 15 | 45 | 18 | 10 |
| 6. Knowledge of adult psychology and development | 5* | 77 | 6 | 59 | 7 | 72 | 3* | 67 | 1* | 70 |
| 7. Evaluation skills (instruction) | 6 | 74 | 7 | 54 | 14 | 65 | 14 | 46 | 14 | 24 |
| 8. Evaluation skills (program) | 9 | 56 | 5* | 65 | 11 | 73 | 11 | 56 | 15 | 21 |
| 9. Team building | 11 | 51 | 15 | 37 | 5* | 74 | 2* | 68 | 11 | 37 |
| 10. Human relations skills | 3* | 82 | 10 | 50 | 4* | 77 | 1* | 66 | 1* | 70 |
| 11. Group dynamics | 5 | 77 | 9 | 52 | 9 | 66 | 3* | 67 | 4* | 50 |
| 12. Knowledge of learning theory | 4* | 78 | 2* | 73 | 12 | 59 | 7 | 62 | 9 | 43 |
| 13. Ability to assess prior student learning | 7 | 72 | 10 | 50 | 16 | 39 | 15 | 45 | 8 | 4 |
| 14. Intervention skills | 8 | 57 | 16 | 33 | 14 | 55 | 9 | 59 | 7 | 46 |
| 15. Manpower planning skills | 19 | 14 | 18 | 27 | 2* | 81 | 12 | 51 | 17 | 15 |
| 16. Knowledge of person/organization interface | 14 | 44 | 11 | 48 | 6 | 73 | 8 | 61 | 6 | 48 |
| 17. Knowledge of organizational characteristics | 15 | 42 | 9 | 52 | 2* | 81 | 3* | 67 | 10 | 42 |
| 18. Teaching practice | 3* | 82 | 14 | 43 | 17 | 38 | 16 | 43 | 16 | 20 |
| 19. Diagnostic skills | 16 | 39 | 8 | 54 | 13 | 57 | 10 | 57 | 5* | 49 |
| 20. Knowledge of training equipment and materials | 1* | 85 | 3* | 70 | 15 | 49 | 13 | 49 | 15 | 21 |
| 21. Knowledge of organizational development theory | 17 | 35 | 12 | 56 | 6 | 73 | 6 | 63 | 12 | 33 |
| 22. Training needs analysis skills | 13 | 45 | 5* | 65 | 8 | 67 | 10 | 57 | 15 | 21 |
| 23. Knowledge of literature of business/education | 10 | 52 | 10 | 50 | 9 | 66 | 13 | 66 | 13 | 31 |

*Ranked as priority competencies.

40

existed not only among a wide range of competencies but in the nature of the educative role which personnel from both domains share.

## Conclusions

This study was undertaken to: (a) assess the interest for baccalaureate and master's level training and development specialists among business, health, government and non-profit organizations; (b) assess the interest in continuing education for training and development specialists; (c) specify competencies needed by training and development specialists; (d) identify the competencies training and development personnel felt were most essential to a postsecondary education program; and (e) identify the background, prior training and associated personnel characteristics of incumbent training and development specialists.

The conclusions which follow were drawn from the assessment's findings:

1. An interest exists for the employment of educators prepared at the master's degree level to serve in training and development positions among health, government, non-profit, and business organizations.

2. A substantial interest exists for the employment of educators prepared at the baccalaureate level to serve in training and development positions among health, government, non-profit, and business organizations.

3. A pressing need exists for continuing education opportunities for persons already employed as training and development specialists.

4. Competencies needed by training and development specialists can be readily categorized and prioritized for use in program development.

5. Though heterogeneous in background and organizational affiliation, training and development specialists understand their roles, functions and educational needs to be similar.

6. Competencies needed by training and development specialists are, in many cases, already delivered by colleges of education through programs geared to traditional audiences. In other cases they may be achievable through adjustments in objectives and contents of existing courses, faculty development, or through other units of the university.

## Implications and Recommendations

The following recommendations are directed to adult educators in collegiate and noncollegiate organizations.

1. Traditional collegiate education programs are adaptable to new audiences of postsecondary educators. Future redesign of degree and non-degree programs would do well to focus on potential markets viewed through the broadest possible definition of professional education.

2. Traditional collegiate education programs need to identify existing curricula which might be appropriately delivered without reference to such specific educational levels as elementary or secondary, or which might be modified to include the full spectrum of human development including adult psychology and learning styles.

3. Collegiate faculty recruited for the future should be considered in light of their experience with or disposition to preparing the broadest range of professional educators via their scholarly concentration.

4. Collegiate institutions would be well served by the conduct of formal needs assessments done among the widest range of professional educators in their respective service areas.

Finally, it can be noted that organizations which represent the various domains of postsecondary education serve little purpose by continuing what has become a historic pattern of separation and isolated development. An appropriate goal for college and university educators, adult education specialists, organizational developers, and training and development specialists, among others, must be increased liaison among respective professional and academic associations. Broudy (15: 699-700) stated that, "Academic guild specialism...is an obstacle to both professional and liberal education in the modern university." The foregoing research, and recognition of congruence between the offerings and needs of two education guilds, implies the need, not only to adapt existing programs but to revitalize the transfer of theory that should characterize all professional education.

## References

1. Briers, James. Capabilities of An Industrial Technologist. Unpublished document, Ohio Bell Telephone Company, February 27, 1978, Cleveland, Ohio.

2. "Core Competencies of Trainers," Canadian Training Methods, December, 1976.

3. Higher Education Program of Studies. (Department of Educational Specialists, The Cleveland State University, Cleveland, Ohio 44115, 1978.)

4. Knowles, Malcolm S. Self-Directed Learning: A Guide for Learners and Teachers. New York: Association Press, 1975.

5. Knowles, Malcolm S. The Adult Learner: A Neglected Species. Houston Gulf Press, 1973.

6. Knowles, Malcolm S. The Modern Practice of Adult Education: Andragogy vs. Pedagogy. New York: Association Press, 1970.

7. Kolb, David. The Learning Style Inventory Technical Manual. Boston, Massachusetts, 1976.

8. Kolb, David and M.S. Plovnick. "The Experiential Learning Theory of Career Development," in New Perspectives in Organizational Careers, J. VanMannen, Editor. New York: John Wiley and Sons, 1976.

9. Methods Identifier for Gaining Knowledge Skills and Attitudes. Unpublished Document, American Airlines, New York, New York, 1966.

10. Nie, Norman S., et al. Statistical Package for The Social Sciences. New York: McGraw Hill Book Co. Inc., 1975.

11. Poppenhagen, Brent W. Postsecondary Education Questionnaire. (Curriculum Development in Postsecondary Education Project, Department of Educational Specialists, The Cleveland State University, Cleveland, Ohio 44115, 1979.)

12. Public Service Commission of Canada. Job Profiles Trainer. Ottawa, Canada, 1975.

13. Public Service Commission of Canada. Personal Development Profile for Skills and Competencies in Training and Education Methodology by B. G. O'Neil. Ottawa, Canada, 1976.

14. U. S. Civil Service Commission. The Employee Development Specialist Curriculum Plan, Bureau of Training, Training Leadership Division, Washington, D.C., November, 1976.

Part Two

## ASPECTS OF EXPERIENTIAL LEARNING

> Experience is not what happens to a man; it
> is what a man does with what happens to him.
>
> - Aldous Huxley

### Introduction

What are the characteristics of experiential learning?  What are some
of its conceptual and empirical foundations?  It is the purpose of Part
Two to discuss these questions as a background for the guidelines for
field experience in Part Three.

Torbert (1972) identifies some of the desired results of learning from
experience as:  "...increasing the effectiveness of action, increasing
the accuracy of...beliefs about patterns in experience, and increasingly
accepting /one's/ emotions as significantly related to situations" (p. 7).
This perspective on experiential learning stresses the importance of
changing at the deepest levels of being.  It is not sufficient to change
behavior as the result of events and encounters; one must change the way
of thinking and feeling about one's self and about the world.

Greenberg and Steinaker and Bell (see Selected Readings on pages 58 and
59) have developed taxonomies of experiential learning.  Their approach is
to view learning from experience as progressing from lower levels of individual consciousness of experience to higher levels of application of
learning through involvement with other people.

The above formulations stress the idea that experiential learning goes
beyond merely subjecting oneself to a variety of situations.  The two
chapters in Part Two deal with some of the emerging models of experiential
learning and discuss current research concerning learning processes in a
number of field-based settings.

Chapter 2

TRADITIONAL AND EMERGING MODELS OF TEACHING,
LEARNING, AND THE ADULT LEARNER

> Personally, I'm always ready to learn although
> I do not always like being taught.
>
> - Winston Churchill

No assumptions have plagued higher education more persistently than
these: "...education occurs as an activity only at certain times in people's lives, in certain institutional settings, at certain times of day,
and in certain few accepted formats" (Carnegie Commission on Higher Education, 1973, p. 4). While these assumptions may characterize the conditions under which teaching typically occurs, they have never represented
fact concerning how students actually learn. Only recently in the postsecondary education community has a genuine concern backed by important
research helped educators to focus on people as active learners rather
than viewing them merely as passive receivers of knowledge.

Until the 1960's very little of what was known about adult learning had
influenced established higher education institutions. Educators had given
less consideration to the concept of learning, which often dealt with
feelings and personal relationships, while more rigorously pursuing the
study of teaching or instructional methodology (Cross, 1977: Dubin &
Taveggia, 1968; Levine, 1978; Milton, 1972; Siegel, 1968).

Kogan (1971) suggested that there existed an "almost total lack of artic-
ulation...between the psychological study of cognition, on the one hand,
and educational research and practice, on the other" (p. 243). Kolb (in
press) reports that learning research had focused primarily on the "...
peripheral norms of academic disciplines (social attitudes, personality
patterns, sex distribution) rather than the pivotal norms governing learning and inquiry" (p. 6). Two factors, one historical, the other psychological, help to explain this phenomenon. Historically, higher education
institutions have passed on to younger generations the intellectual tradi-
tions and achievements of the past. Colleges and universities have,
therefore, transmitted knowledge in their effort to prepare the young for
adulthood. Under these conditions, teaching was recognized as the process
by which cognitive knowledge was transmitted, placing greater emphasis
upon the study of expository teaching and receptive learning. Traditional
college students, aged 17 to 22, were characterized as consumers rather
than co-producers of knowledge.

Approaches to the design of instruction from both the perspectives of cognitive and behaviorist psychologies[1] have traditionally resulted in prescriptions emphasizing the sequencing of predetermined content with the goal of optimizing various educational outcomes (e.g., speed of acquisition, retention, transfer). In recent years, the study of individual differences in cognitive and affective learning styles has gained the attention of learning psychologists. Even now, however, instruction in colleges and universities does not adequately take into account differences among students as learners. Most practitioners in higher educational institutions have not had sufficient opportunity to refocus their view of the student from that of passive receiver to that of active, integrating learner.

## An Emerging Learning Model

Experiential approaches to learning have been gaining understanding and respect in postsecondary education over the past decade. In the tradition of John Dewey, Kurt Lewin, and Carl Rogers, education (even _higher_ education) is being seen to involve not only subject content, but the growth processes of the learners as well. Weathersby (1978) has pointed out that "people's learning interests are embedded in their personal histories, in their visions of who they are in the world and in what they can do and want to do" (p. 19). Mere intellectual knowledge is being increasingly recognized as sterile without the commitment of the learners to give it vitality.

Stemming from his experience and research with group-based learning, Blake (1960) advanced a four-phase learning model: dilemma-invention-feedback-generalization. This inductive approach was ideally suited to learning about oneself in the context of group dynamics. Its applicability to cognitive learning in more formal educational settings, however, was discounted for many years.

Hampden-Turner (1971) proposed a model of psycho-social development which pictured all human growth and development as a series of risk-taking initiatives toward the world in general and toward particular individuals. Feedback from each such foray would result in a new integration of a person's identity at a higher level of complexity. Applied to the field of education, this model pictured self-initiated learning episodes resulting in higher and higher levels of educational attainment and personal competence.

Research, theory, and practice in adult education (Gross, 1977; Kidd, 1959; Knowles, 1973; Smith, Aker & Kidd, 1970), while considered irrelevant to higher education for many years, have recently become a major part of the foundation for the myriad of "nontraditional" higher educational programs. Several other factors, too, have helped bolster the active and self-directing role of the learner. For one thing, the realization of the prophecies of the futurists (Morphet & Jesser, 1968; Shane, 1973; Toffler, 1970) regarding the exponential growth rate of knowledge has finally exposed the passive role of the learner as ineffective and obsolete. The proliferation of alternative routes to continuing education under the auspices of organizations such as business and industry, the military, and proprietary schools has also caused administrators and

---

[1] See, for example, Ausubel (1968) and Gagne (1970).

faculty members in higher educational institutions to rethink their missions and approaches to learning. The current shortage of students in the traditional age group reinforces the other trends mentioned.

At the graduate level, traditional learning models have persisted, by and large, although internships, practicums, and field-based courses have been part of professional graduate education for years. There is a growing movement, however, toward involving graduate students more actively in learning projects and in emphasizing experiential learning strategies (Poppenhagen, 1979). Colleges and universities across the country have begun to offer graduate programs which credit learning activities of an experiential nature (Innovative...Directory, 1976; Somers, 1979). Poppenhagen and Byxbee (in press) have discussed the changing faculty roles fostered by emerging learning models.

The results of recent research suggest a future where many styles of learning will be institutionally desirable. No longer will all participants in higher learning be subjected solely to directive teaching aimed at cognitive processes alone. Institutions will not feel compelled to minimize the developmental achievements which have accompanied adult life. Learning will be recognized as intellectual and experiential, resulting from the integration of cognitive and developmental processes.

Chapter 3

## DESIGNS FOR ACTIVE LEARNING

> Experience is a hard teacher because she
> gives the test first - the lesson after-
> wards.
>
> - Vernon Law

In the field of experiential learning in postsecondary settings, three
current approaches to investigation suggest the richness of efforts to
achieve understanding and to improve practice. The first approach, by
Lenore Borzak and Barbara Hursh, centers around the study of students'
cognitive development and changes in self-perception stemming from experiential learning. Another thrust, by Allen Tough, focuses on the exploration of strategies and processes that adults employ in designing and
carrying out active learning programs of their own choosing. David Kolb,
in a third perspective, deals with an investigation of individual learning styles and their interrelationships within a theory of experiential
learning.

Borzak and Hursh (1977; 1979) suggest that experiential learning may,
paradoxically, foster many of the qualities of learning traditionally
sought in classroom-based programs of liberal education. Focusing their
research on undergraduate students in communications and community service, these authors explore the cognitive and emotional consequences of
field-based internship experiences.

One desirable outcome of liberal education is that a person become aware
of and know how to employ multiple perspectives in dealing with personal
and societal problems. Another key learning result of liberally educated
persons is that they be able to achieve mutually satisfying and productive
relationships with others in work and social settings. These two processes - flexibility, on the one hand, and mutual influence on the other -
are respectively termed decentering and reciprocity by Borzak and Hursh
(1977). They find that the combination of decentering and reciprocity
"produce a synergistic effect, with both affective and cognitive outcomes"
(p. 4). Two of these important outcomes are an increased sense of competence and the ability to think holistically. Not only are these outcomes
desirable from a liberal education point of view, but they form the basis
for competent professional practice as well. Perhaps of equal importance
are several related results of the processes of decentering and reciprocity: an improved attitude toward learning about oneself and others, an
increased ability to solve problems, more effectiveness in interpersonal

communication, and the ability to integrate material from diverse sources (Borzak & Hursh, 1977, p. 4).

Experiential learning - that is, educational experiences which include components of both academic and vocational responsibilities - often produce role conflict in students due to differing expectations from the college and the work site. In one reported study, students attempted to deal with this conflict in four ways: (1) emphasize the college perspective, (2) emphasize the work site perspective, (3) reject both perspectives, and (4) blend or integrate the two perspectives (Borzak & Hursh, 1977, p. 10). Students who adopted the fourth approach developed "meta-perspectives," (Hursh & Borzak, 1979, p. 76) and they were able to utilize the decentering process to a high degree. The key factor, according to Borzak and Hursh, in being able to integrate multiple perspectives was the degree of reciprocity present at the work site. They found that, "in the absence of reciprocal influence, students will be less likely to achieve a feeling of internship success" (1977, p. 10).

Decentering and reciprocity are interrelated processes, it would appear, that have a direct bearing on the quantity and quality of active learning. Experiencing and learning how to employ these two processes resulted not only in cognitive development but in a strengthening of self-concept. Students saw themselves as more active than passive, more autonomous than controlled, and more responsible than powerless.

Allen Tough, a teacher and researcher from the Ontario Institute for Studies in Education in Toronto, Canada, has focused his investigations on how adults engage in self-developed learning projects. He has determined that "the typical adult conducts five of them per year, altogether spending 500 hours on major learning efforts" (Tough, 1978, p. 9). Moreover, while some of these learning projects take place in formal classroom settings, "more than 70 percent are self-planned, and others rely on friends and peer groups" (1978, p. 9).

In explaining why so many people elect to learn on their own rather than making use of coursework developed by colleges and other institutions, Tough (1979), cites the major study by P. R. Penland. Penland (1977) surveyed adults from all over the United States and found that the most frequently encountered responses regarding the popularity of self-initiated learning had to do not with lack of money or transportation problems, but with the desire of learners to set their own pace, to employ their own learning style, and to structure the experience according to their own learning needs (Penland, 1979).

Even though learners may initiate their own projects, the approaches to planning the details of content, sequence, and duration of learning episodes within the projects may differ. Tough (1979) identifies four planning methods, or "planners": (1) the learner himself; (2) a non-human resource, such as programmed instruction or audiotape; (3) another person, such as a peer or tutor; and (4) a group of persons with whom the learner is joined (pp. 78-79).

In order to maximize the potential of adult learning projects, learners must engage in a number of steps and develop several skills related to self-directed learning. Some of these are planning skills, such as "deciding the specific activities, methods, resources, or equipment for learning," or "deciding where to learn." Other skills involve the implementation of the learning plan. Examples are "deciding the pace at which to

50

proceed," "finding time for the learning," "setting specific deadlines or intermediate targets," and "obtaining the desired resources." In addition to planning and implementation skills, the self-directed learner needs evaluation competencies such as "estimating the current level of his knowledge or skill," and "detecting any factor that has been blocking or hindering this learning" (Tough, 1979, pp. 95-96).

What motivates adults to spend so much time and effort in pursuing self-directed learning projects? Tough (1979) has stated that "the benefits anticipated by the learner are not only intellectual, cognitive, and material; many are emotional or psychological, including pleasure, satisfaction, self-esteem, impressing others, and receiving praise" (pp. 45-46). Tough's research seems to validate the assertions of Maslow (1965) and McGregor (1960) that persons naturally seek self-actualization and they will put forth great effort in the pursuit of goals which they find meaningful.

A third researcher and theorist, David Kolb, from Case Western Reserve University, has devoted many years to the study of adult learning styles. Taking as their point of departure the experiential learning model developed by Kurt Lewin and his associates, Kolb and Fry (1975) define two primary dimensions of the learning process: quality of experiencing and level of activity. They maintain that "learning requires abilities that are polar opposites and the learner, as a result, must continually choose which set of learning abilities he will bring to bear in any specific learning situation" (p. 36).

At one end of the quality-of-experiencing continuum is Concrete Experience (CE) and at the other end is Abstract Conceptualization (AC). Persons whose mode of learning tends toward CE rely heavily on feeling-based judgments and prefer to become involved with other people in specific learning episodes. Learners tending towards AC, on the other hand, are more rational and conceptual in their approach and prefer symbolic rather than personal learning interactions (Kolb, 1976).

The level-of-activity dimension has at its one extremity Active Experimentation (AE) and at the other, Reflective Observation (RO). Active experimenters have a "doing" orientation to learning which involves taking action and modifying behavior in the light of success or failure. Reflective observers prefer careful observation rather than involvement, and they learn best by thinking about and comparing ideas.

If the two learning dimensions are seen as the axes of a grid, four learning styles can be defined based on the emphasis one places on CE or AC, on the one dimension, and on AE or RO, on the other. Thus, a high reliance on CE and AE is characteristic of the Accommodator - one whose learning style stresses risk-taking and intuitive problem solving. Emphasis on AC and RO defines the Assimilator learning style, where theory building, inductive reasoning, and conceptualizing are key learning activities. The Converger's learning style, defined by high AC and AE, stresses the practical application of ideas, while the Diverger's style, high CE and RO, tends to utilize imagination, creativity, and generalization to a great degree (Kolb, 1976). See Figure 1 for the experiential learning model.

Kolb (1976) has developed a self-assessment instrument, the Learning Style Inventory (LSI), which enables a person to identify his/her patterns of learning in terms of the two major dimensions and four learning styles.

51

# Figure 1. The Experiential Learning Model and Learning Styles

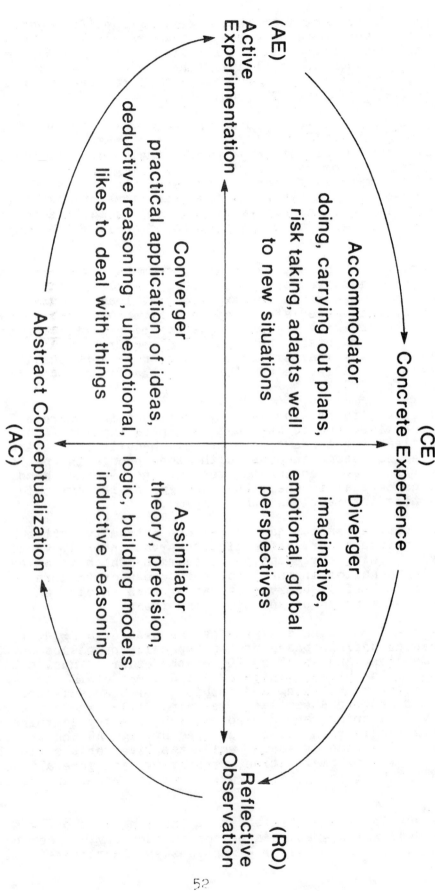

(CE)
Concrete Experience

Accommodator
doing, carrying out plans,
risk taking, adapts well
to new situations

Diverger
imaginative,
emotional, global
perspectives

(AE)
Active
Experimentation

Converger
practical application of ideas,
deductive reasoning , unemotional,
likes to deal with things

Assimilator
theory, precision,
logic, building models,
inductive reasoning

Abstract Conceptualization
(AC)

(RO)
Reflective
Observation

Based On: David Kolb, BUILDING A LEARNING COMMUNITY: A START-UP PROGRAM FOR ADULT LEARNERS (Washington, D.C.: National Training and Development Service, 1976). Summary of learning style types inserted by authors.

A good deal of research with the LSI has been conducted by Kolb and others regarding the learning styles of adults in a variety of settings (Kolb, in press; Kolb & Fry, 1975).

Theoretically, according to Kolb (1975), although persons early in life tend to favor one of the four learning styles, the maturation process over years should enable them to develop a more complex approach to learning. In other words, "growth proceeds from a state of embeddedness, defensiveness, dependency, and reaction, to a state of self-actualization, independence, proaction, and self-direction" (p. 41).

In the light of this developmental concept, the design of learning experiences for adults becomes an opportunity and a challenge to enlarge the learning repertoires of the participants. As Kolb (in press) points out, "continuous life long learning requires learning how to learn and this involves appreciation of and competence in diverse approaches to creating, manipulating, and communicating knowledge" (p. 44).

In Chapter 9 of this volume, many of the concepts presented in this chapter will again be encountered. Chapter 9 reports the results of a research study involving participants in an internship experience designed in consonance with the ideas of Hursh and Borzak, Tough, and Kolb. The study examined the extent to which participants were able to move toward self-direction in learning, to begin to view problems from a variety of perspectives (decentering), and to learn to build mutually productive relationships (reciprocity). The study also investigated the relationships between Kolb's four learning styles and participants' development of various self-directed learning skills.

What impact will the models of experiential education ultimately hold for postsecondary education? Their prescriptions are ambitious. Hursh and Borzak confront the very heart of higher education's tradition when they identify experiential learning as capable of fostering many of the liberal qualities usually associated with directed classroom programs. Equally dramatic is Tough's description of how adults learn. This new understanding may finally bring into being student centered reform long predicted for postsecondary education. As if to validate these prescriptions, Kolb describes the theoretical tools to make experiential learning a key to expanded learning repertoires for the future, not only in the tradition of liberal learning, but for adult learning throughout life. Separately, these models represent pieces of the emerging views held by many educators. Collectively, they provide a substantial foundation for program development and change. It was on the basis of these models that the design for experiential learning presented in this volume was formulated.

Selected Readings

AN ANDRAGOGICAL LEARNING APPROACH
TO GRADUATE PROFESSIONAL EDUCA-
TION*
Ernest M. Schuttenberg

This paper enumerates
four major assumptions
of andragogy (adult
learning) and points
out their implications
for the design and con-
duct of learning exper-
iences for graduate
students in profes-
sional schools.

**GRADUATE** PROFESSIONAL SCHOOLS
of education, medicine, law, engineering, and other fields are
responsible to society for the
caliber of their educational
programs. In order for their
graduates to serve the community
more effectively, schools and
faculties must examine the nature
of the learning experiences they
provide. Traditionally, students
in college and graduate school
have been taught with methods
more appropriate for children

---

*Reprinted with permis-
sion of the publisher
from Improving College
and University Teaching
Year Book 1975, Oregon
State University Press,
pp. 227-236.

and youth. Overconcern with mastery of predetermined facts and
ideas, over reliance upon the
recollection of details on examinations, and under utilization of
student knowledge and learning
resources may be appropriate for
a group of learners who are passive, unimaginative, and unsophis-
ticated. But most students in
graduate professional schools are
adults who may hold jobs and have
families, and who are already
active contributors to the welfare
of their communities. If such
students are preparing themselves
to serve society at an even more
complex level, should not their
program of preparation for such
service actively involve them in
their own learning? As Werdell
argues, "The institution can develop self-directed learners only
by innovating new teaching and
learning models through which
students can learn their own
learning process, learn what they
want to learn, and learn how to
communicate this to other people."[1]
This paper discusses some of the
characteristics of adult learners
and examines implications of these
for the design and conduct of graduate professional courses.

Pedagogy and Andragogy

Pedagogy (from the Greek words
for "child" and "leader") is the
art and science of teaching.
Through history, those considered
most in need of teaching were
children. The body of knowledge
that has accumulated relative to
teaching and learning has been,
until recently, geared to the educational needs of children and
youth. When adults went to school
from time to time, the same principles and methods of instruction
were applied to their learning
programs.
The second half of the 20th century, however, has become the era
of the adult learner. In the last
decade the future oriented curriculum has been stressed, due in

55

large part to the ever accelerating fund of knowledge in almost every field. In what ways do adult learners differ from younger learners, and how can adult graduate students in the professions best be aided in developing learning strategies for dealing with future problems and planning future opportunities?

In 1968, Malcolm Knowles introduced the term andragogy[2] (from the Greek words for "man" and "leader") to distinguish adult learning theories and technologies from those developed principally for and related to children. Table 1 points up four differing assumptions about the learner related to pedagogical and andragogical practice.

Table 1. Pedagogical and Andragogical Assumptions about Learners*

Factors
A. Self Concept of Learner
B. Role of Experience
C. Readiness to Learn
D. Orientation to Learning

Pedagogy
A. Dependent on "experts" for learning
B. Limited experience to relate to new learning
C. Motivation to learn comes from academic pressures
D. Subject-centered and answer-centered focus

Andragogy
A. Increasing self-direction in learning
B. Broad experience available as learning resource
C. Motivation to learn comes from perceived problems and vocational needs
D. Problem-centered and question-centered focus.

---

* Based on Malcolm S. Knowles, The Adult Learner: A Neglected Species (Houston, Tex.: Gulf Publishing Company, 1973), pp. 45-49.

Based upon these four andragogical assumptions, there are a number of implications for the design and conduct of courses and other learning programs for adults in graduate professional programs. Table 2 lists some of these implications.

Table 2. Implications of Andragogical Assumptions for Course Design and Conduct**

ASSUMPTION A: Changes in Self-concept Towards Increasing Self-Direction

Implications:

A1. Students participate in self-diagnosis of learning needs.

A2. Students and teachers share in the planning process for learning.

A3. Students and teachers share responsibility for personal and group learning.

A4. Students and teachers share in the evaluation of learning.

A5. Teacher solicits student contributions.

A6. Teacher and students share spirit of mutuality as joint inquirers.

A7. Teacher makes efforts to know students as individuals.

A8. Teacher fosters psychological climate of acceptance and support.

A9. Teacher fosters friendly and informal atmosphere.

ASSUMPTION B: Role of Experience As a Learning Resource

Implications:

B1. Passive, information-transmittal teaching methods are minimized; active, experiential learning methods are emphasized.

B2.  Practical application is built into the learning experience.

B3.  Collaboration with other class members is fostered rather than competition.

ASSUMPTION C:  Readiness to Learn What Is Perceived as Essential

Implications:

C1.  Students are encouraged to relate learnings to their career needs and plans.

C2.  Students are encouraged to work and share with others who have similar interests and needs.

ASSUMPTION D.  Orientation to Learning as Problem Solving

Implications:

D1.  Subject matter presentations are flexible enough to accommodate student concerns.

D2.  Student problem areas are identified and dealt with.

---

** Adapted from Malcolm S. Knowles, The Modern Practice of Adult Education: Andragogy Versus Pedagogy (New York:  Association Press, 1970), pp. 39-49.

A major implication is that a new focus needs to be placed on the objectives of learning.  While it is important for students in graduate professional courses to master and retain areas of course content, it is also essential that they learn behaviors they will need in order to function as professionals in a complex and rapidly changing society where content may become obsolete within a few months or years after graduation.  Table 3 lists ten meta objectives, based on andragogical assumptions that should supplement content mastery objectives in graduate professional courses.

Table 3.  Meta Objectives Based on Andragogical Assumptions

1.  To identify important problems to be dealt with.

2.  To set challenging personal learning goals.

3.  To take the responsibility for attaining learning goals or for modifying them in the light of relevant new information.

4.  To use a variety of appropriate written and human resources effectively in conducting research in problem areas.

5.  To relate personal philosophy and values to issues in the field of study.

6.  To state one's position clearly on controversial issues in the field of study and to support that position with valid data.

7.  To listen to and learn from the ideas of others.

8.  To work collaboratively with colleagues in increasing personal and group learning.

9.  To diagnose strengths and weaknesses and to make plans to build on strengths and to improve weaknesses.

10.  To risk making mistakes and to learn from mistakes made.

FOOTNOTES

1 Philip Runkel, Roger Harrison, and Margaret Runkel (eds.), The Changing College Classroom (San Francisco, Cal.:  Jossey-Bass, Inc., 1969), p. 14.

2 Malcolm S. Knowles, The Modern Practice of Adult Education: Andragogy Versus Pedagogy (New York:  Association Press, 1970), pp. 305-306.

CATEGORIES OF THE EXPERIENTIAL
TAXONOMY*
Norman W. Steinaker
M. Robert Bell

1.0 EXPOSURE: Consciousness of an experience. This involves two levels of exposure and a readiness for further experience.

    1.1 SENSORY: Through various sensory stimuli one is exposed to the possibility of an experience.

    1.2 RESPONSE: Peripheral mental reaction to sensory stimuli. At this point, one rejects or accepts further interaction with the experience.

    1.3 READINESS: At this level one has accepted the experience and anticipates participation in it.

2.0 PARTICIPATION: The decision to become physically a part of an experience. There are two levels of interaction within this category.

---

*Reprinted with permission from The Experiential Taxonomy: A New Approach to Teaching and Learning, New York: Academic Press, Inc., 1979, pp. 10-11.

    2.1 REPRESENTATION: Reproducing, mentally and/or physically, an existing mental image of the experience, that is, through visualizing, role playing, or dramatic play. This can be done in two ways:

        2.1.1 COVERTLY: as a private, personal "walk through" rehearsal.

        2.1.2 OVERTLY: in a small or large group or interaction, that is, in the classroom or playground.

    2.2 MODIFICATION: With the input of past personal activities, the experience develops and grows. As there is a personal input in the participation, one moves from role player to active participant.

3.0 IDENTIFICATION: The coming together of the learner and the idea (objective) in an emotional and intellectual context for the achievement of the objective.

    3.1 REINFORCEMENT: As the experience is modified and repeated, it is reinforced through a decision to identify with the experience.

    3.2 EMOTIONAL: The participant becomes emotionally identified with the experience. It becomes "my experience."

    3.3 PERSONAL: The participant moves from an emotional identification to an intellectual commitment that involves a

rational decision to
identify.

    3.4 SHARING: Once the proc-
ess of identification is
accomplished, the partic-
ipant begins to share the
experience with others,
as an important factor in
his life. This kind of
positive sharing continues
into and through Category
4.0 (internalization).

4.0 INTERNALIZATION: The participant moves from identification
to internalization when the
experience begins to affect
the life-style of the participant. There are two levels
of this category.

    4.1 EXPANSION: The experi-
ence enlarges into many
aspects of the partici-
pant's life, changing
attitudes and activities.
When these changes become
more than temporary, the
participant moves to the
next category.

    4.2 INTRINSIC: The experi-
ence characterizes the
participant's life-style
more consistently than
during the expansion level.

5.0 DISSEMINATION: The experience
moves beyond internalization to
the dissemination of the experience. It goes beyond the positive sharing that began at
Level 3.0 and involves two levels of activity.

    5.1 INFORMATIONAL: The par-
ticipant informs others
about the experience and
seeks to stimulate others
to have an equivalent ex-
perience through descrip-
tive and personalized
sharing.

    5.2 HOMILETIC: The partici-
pant sees the experience
as imperative for others.

## THE COMMUNITY AS A LEARNING RESOURCE*
Ellie Greenberg

    The rich human resources
within a community can be
tapped to provide students
with the needed balance
between theory and exper-
ience. A framework for
such programs comes
from learning theory.

### Introduction

    The concepts and models describ-
ed in this article have been utilized by the author for program
development purposes in a number
of organizations and presentations, such as:
    1969 to 1971: as a portion of
a workshop to train community
agency volunteers, through the
Arapahoe Institute for Community Development, Littleton,
Colorado.
    1971 to present: in the devel-
opment of the design for the
University Without Walls Program at Loretto Heights College, Denver, Colorado.

*Reprinted with permis-
sion of the author
from the Journal of
Experiential Education,
Vol. 1, No. 2, 1978,
pp. 22-25.

1973: as a presentation prepared for western European educators attending a conference at the University of Vienna, Austria. The conference was one of four such events held in Europe in 1972 and 1973, sponsored and organized by the Union for Experimenting Colleges and Universities, Ohio, under a grant from UNESCO.

1973: as a portion of a presentation prepared for a conference on Cable TV, attended by persons from the fields of business, education, government, and communications at Denver University, sponsored by the Denver Research Institute, Denver, Colorado,

and in other workshops and presentations over the past ten years.

The intent of presenting these ideas in the Journal for Experiential Education is to provide one conceptual framework, which may aid practitioners who are committed to combining experiential learning with theoretical learning in various educational environments.

Oftentimes, we are able to articulate a belief or philosophy in regard to experiential learning, but are less able to be clear about the theories which undergird our beliefs. In addition, we need to be able to design systems within our projects and schools which reflect coherent, comprehensive, and practical applications of our philosophies. The ideas and models presented here can be utilized in schools, colleges, and community agencies-- in any program which has a commitment to utilizing the Community as a Learning Resource.

There are three essential elements which must be conceptualized in order to use effectively the Community as a Learning Resource: 1) learning, 2) the community, and 3) learning resources.

## What is Learning?

Throughout the ages, many "theories of learning" have been developed and defended. "How people learn" has been a pre-occupation of philosophers, psychologists, educators, behavioral scientists, and others since the beginning of written history. Since we are not certain which of these learning theories is correct, we tend to be eclectic in our approaches to learners and to education, while we search the literature for conceptual designs that match or explain our own experiences as educators. Which theories we choose may not be as important as choosing something. Each of us must develop some way of thinking about how learning takes place. If we have no framework for how learning occurs, it will not be possible for us to design coherent educational programs for young learners or adult learners. If we have no framework, what we design will be will-o'-the-wisp, fragile, personal bits of philosophy upon which programs are built, which cannot survive the challenges of intellectual debate nor political trends. These programs may serve the personal biases of the program designers, but will not serve the learners well. And, they will be difficult to sustain or integrate into ongoing institutions.

So, even while we continue to search for greater understanding of the learning process, we must continue to teach and help others to learn, in spite of the knowledge that the final answers are not yet in.

One Learning Level Theory, the notion of balancing theory and practice, is as old as the idea of education itself. Socrates, Leonardo, Michelangelo, and countless apprentices and interns throughout the centuries have learned, identified with, and achieved competencies and skills through personal associations with "masters." The great European university tutorial and mentor systems preceded the lecture halls, and persist today. The apprentice systems and the medieval guilds have grown into contemporary forms and are still utilized throughout the world. And, as America dedicated itself to free public education and the socialization of the 19th and 20th century immigrants, our mass education system substituted vicarious classroom instruction in volume to the exclusion of personal, experiential learning methods. In our efforts to develop an informed democratic citizenry, we have prolonged an adolescent dependency, placing the learner in a passive, third-party role. Whereas we were once experience-rich and theory-poor, our youth is now theory-rich and experience-poor. The experiential education movement is an attempt to right the balance once again, to combine theory and practice, making use of "the best of both worlds," the academic and the community. There is no substitute for experience. Well-planned experience, coupled with serious study, reflection, and interchange with other learners can provide the best combination of educational experiences. What is real is always preferred to what is vicarious. There is no such thing as simulated living. Too long has education concentrated upon the vicarious, the simulated, instead of the reality of experiential problem-solving. The experiential education movement attempts to reverse this trend.

A basic assumption of the Learning Level Theory is that a desirable goal for students (and, therefore, for all contemporary responsible adult world citizens) is the ability of the individual to effect positive changes in the institutions and systems of the community and the society, as well as in his or her own life. This assumption pre-supposes that 1) we value persons being in control of their own individual lives, thereby reducing victimization by a rapidly changing mass technological society; and 2) that we value the "change agent" or person who uses his or her knowledge and skills to improve the institutions of society.

Educators must have a vision of what the ideal desired outcomes of learning might be in order to design any learning experience. And, in order to define the levels of competency a student has at the outset of a learning experience, to help set the goals to be achieved, and to measure those achievements, a Learning Level Theory is offered.

There are seven Learning Levels: 1) No consciousness, 2) Awareness, 3) Theoretical knowledge, 4) Experience, 5) Reflection, synthesis, and generalization, 6) Commitment and action, and 7) Influence on others. Learning levels can also be determined by identifying various Role Categories and Resultant Behaviors.

## Learning Level Theory Illustrated

The example of Resultant Behaviors used in Figure #1 is related to the issue of Day Care Centers. Other examples are possible. Any academic discipline, community issue, or job skill can be specified by appropriate resultant behaviors at each level, sometimes called "behavioral objectives." This model may be adapted to a variety of fields of human endeavor and may aid in making the progress of students explicit. The model may be used to be specific about competencies, supplementing or replacing "time-spent", credits, grades or other inventions as measures of learning. It can be especially useful in aiding students to define their roles in community-based experiential learning activities, and can give help to faculty and resource persons in their evaluations and assessments of student learning and performance. Each level can

Figure 1.  LEARNING LEVEL THEORY

| | Learning Levels | Role Categories | Resultant Behaviors |
|---|---|---|---|
| 0. | No consciousness | Apathy | None |
| 1. | Awareness | Observer | Reads newspaper article.  Visits day care center. |
| 2. | Theoretical knowledge | Vicarious learner | Reads books or studies.  Attends meetings on day care. Takes courses on Early Childhood Development. |
| 3. | Experience | Intern apprentice | Volunteers at day care center. Lobbies for day care center. |
| 4. | Reflection, generalization and synthesis | Programmer or program leader | Teaches regularly at day care center. |
| 5. | Commitment and action | Supervisor | Directs day care center. Plans and/or develops a day care center model. |
| 6. | Influence on others | Policy-maker, with power | Serves on Governor's Day Care Center Committee.  Is an officer in day care center organization.  Sets statewide day care policies. |

---

be broken down into finer sub-categories of learning, roles and behaviors.  The theory is more orderly than the reality of our actual learning.  We often skip levels and find a need to return to a former level.  In this sense, it is a theoretical model, useful to guide our real planning, but not to predict it entirely.  In another sense, it is ideal.  Imagine if all policy-makers actually proceeded through all six levels before being given the responsibility for major decision-making. It is useful to think of each of our students as potential policy-makers.  How carefully we might teach them!

This Learning Level Theory can be useful in establishing "where a student is" at the outset of a learning experience, on the yard-stick or continuum of learning, and can provide a guide for specifying the objectives and expected outcomes of each learning experience.  It may be especially useful to employ such a guide with adult learners, who are often experience-rich and theory-poor.  It can be equally useful with young learners, aiding them to distinguish between levels of sophistication in their experiential learning.  All learning experiences are not alike nor equally valuable.

The important balances to maintain are:  theory and experience, doing and reflection, learning and meaning, cognition and personal growth, specificity and generalization.  Like a see-saw, we move from one to the other throughout life, as we continue to learn, develop, and establish our values and competencies.

University Without Walls
Organizing Concept #5

"There are many ways in
which students can learn. The
traditional college class in
which the professor lectures
or leads discussion is one way.
Students also learn from their
own first-hand experiences,
from friends, from employers
or supervisors, from televis-
ion, radio, films, newspapers,
magazines, books, travel, and
interaction in various cultures
and sub-cultures."[1]

What is a Community? One Model

Since human beings have lived
in groups and organized themselves to trade goods and services, communities have developed
as intra- and inter-dependent
units. In every contemporary
western community there are iden-
tifiable sub-systems. That is,
there are functional units of
community life which are developed and organized to serve the
needs of the people of the community. Most contemporary western communities can be analyzed
as containing sixteen major sub-
systems, which provide the goods
and services required by 20th
century people. The relative
power and importance of these
sub-systems may vary from culture
to culture, but they seem to be
present in one form or another.
As cultures vary, so the relative
influences of the systems vary.
Also, each sub-system is related
to every other sub-system, so
that the quality and nature of
the interfaces between the sub-
systems affect the quality of
community life. We often define
these interfaces as communication.

[1]The University Without Walls: A
First Report: Union for Experimenting Colleges and Universities, 1973.

The figure below is a 'map' of
the contemporary community in
terms of its institutions. It
is one view of the institutions
or sub-systems of a modern community. These sub-systems manage
the delivery of goods and services,
both public and private, to individuals who live in geo-political
areas, communities, or physical
places.
There are four major clusters
of sub-systems:
1) Safety sub-systems,* which
are highly organized, hierarchical
in structure and are meant to
respond instantaneously.
2) Political/Economic sub-
systems,** which are relatively
highly organized, relatively hierarchical in structure, and respond
rapidly.
3) Public Service sub-systems,***
which are moderately organized,
somewhat less hierarchical in
structure, and respond relatively
slowly.
4) Human Development sub-
systems,**** which are not highly
organized, are relatively non-
hierarchical, are the least well
developed, and respond slowly.

The Community -- an institutional
model:

*
Disaster Response: Military &
Civil Defense
*
Fire & Civil Protection
**
Government
***
Information Procurement &
Processes: Census,
Research, Data
*
Administration of Justice:
Courts, Police
***
Natural Resources: Water,
Air, Waste
***
Energy Production:
Power, Fuel

63

****
Religion:  Churches,
    Synagogues
****
Recreation:  Parks,
    Engertainment,
Community groups
**
Economics:  Industry,
Commerce, & Business
***
Communications:  Mass
    Media, TV, Radio,
    Press, Books
****
Health & Social Services:
    Medical, mental,
    public & private
***
Transportation:  Airplanes,
    boats, trains, buses,
    autos & thoroughfares
****
Cultural Arts:  Music,
    Theatre, Art
****
Family

This institutional view of our
community can give us a mental
framework through which to organize the seemingly infinite "Yellow Pages" of our community.  We
can decide how to organize learning experiences, how to inventory
experiential learning opportunities, how to think about vocational preparation, how to plan for
social action, even how to construct community-based curricula.
    Some field-based education pro-
grams have catalogued and constructed an Inventory of Learning
Resources in terms of these real
life sub-systems, rather than
along the lines of traditional,
segmented academic disciplines.
Either approach can work.  Both
have been tried.  Disciplines
and sub-systems can be interwoven.
    Each sub-system can be subdi-
vided to provide categories within
it.  Example:  Education can be
subdivided into day care, early
childhood, elementary, secondary,
vocational, undergraduate, graduate, adult, alternative.  A complete inventory would then provide
a system to catalogue, computerize,

or file any and all learning opportunities, in terms of their
direct relevance to the continually changing employment market
and students' interests.  Using
this visual aid or "map" of the
community, students can be helped
to see the relationship between
theoretical studies, experiential
learning, and potential employment
areas.  Students could also be
encouraged to understand and be
familiar with the inter-relation-
ships between the sub-systems,
their interfaces, their relative
power, and the individual's role
in shaping and changing the community and its institutions.
    By placing the regular academic
disciplines and subjects within
the real-life community sub-systems,
both for theoretical study and experiential learning, curricula can
be designed and understood in terms
of their real-life applications.
Inventories of Learning Resources
can supplement libraries in efforts
to organize community resources for
use by both learners and teachers.

What are Learning Resources?  One
Example -- The UWW Inventory of
Learning Resources

    "Many persons outside the reg-
ular educational institution can
contribute significantly to students' undergraduate experience.
Limiting educational leadership
to the faculty of the colleges
and universities deprives students of working with those men
and women who are outstanding
in their own roles and able to
give students the most up-to-
date viewpoints.  Any society
should include among its educators its best artists, scientists, writers, musicians, dan-
cers, physicians, lawyers, cler-
gymen, industrialists, financiers,
and other specialists."[2]

[2]The University Without Walls; A
First Report:  Union for Experimenting Colleges and Universities, 1973.

64

Within such an Inventory of Learning Resources there can be a variety of kinds of learning opportunities. Resources for learning alone and in one-to-one relationships, usually theoretical in nature, are often called Independent Studies. Examples of these resources are: libraries, books, films, audio cassettes, videotapes, TV, art lessons, music instruction, and most important, resource persons to supervise these studies.

Resources for learning by modeling and practical application, experiential in nature, may be called Independent Field Projects. Examples of these resources are: apprenticeships, internships, practicums, laboratory projects, employment-related projects, volunteer activities, outdoor education, and travel. Resource persons are often selected to supervise, guide, and evaluate these projects.

Resources for learning in groups, which are offered by non-school agencies, businesses, and organizations, can be called Seminars-in-the-Field. Some examples are: special workshops, conferences, and in-service training. The leaders or instructors of these seminars can be identified as resource persons.

Resources for learning in conventional classrooms, courses offered by a variety of schools and colleges, can, of course, also be utilized. These resources provide theoretical group learning experiences, far beyond the capability of any one school or campus to provide.

The essential ideas behind these diverse learning experiences are that legitimate learning can take place in many situations, with many different persons functioning as teachers, alone, in one-to-one situations, in small groups, and in large groups, integrated learning requires and synthesizes both theory and practice, and utilizes the broadest

range of resources available to the learner. Every community contains skilled and talented persons who enjoy teaching others, but whose primary occupation is outside the academic community. These resource persons frequently enjoy the opportunity to play the role of mentor and teacher, and devote extraordinary amounts of time to students, both as volunteers and with remuneration. These persons include: doctors, attorneys, artists, professors, linguists, business persons, social service agency personnel, government officials and employees, musicians, psychologists, nurses, scientists, community developers, teachers, artisans, writers, and the like. Virtually any and all professions and skills may be represented in the inventory.

How each project, school, or college can organize and legitimize these learning resources varies. The role relationships and responsibilities of regular faculty vis-a-vis community learning resources must be clearly defined and accepted. The ages and purposes of the learners will also define the parameters of community-based learning. The degree of individualization and standardization within the program will also determine the uses of those resources. These are subjects for other articles.

In Summary...

...If an educational program provides a theory of learning and defines specific competencies to be gained--and,
...if the community sub-systems are understood and used in cooperation with the academic disciplines--and,
...if persons, events, experiences, media, courses and other learning resources are identified and catalogued--then...
The Community can function as a total Learning Resource for

persons -- helping them to become independent, responsible, and creative life-long learners. In this way, schools and communities can be interwoven. Education, then, will be made of the stuff of life; and life, as it is lived, will be inseparable from the process of education. Becoming one, the Learning Society can become a reality in this century. For our youth will learn how to develop and obtain access to the community; our adults will seek recurrent education throughout their lives, and our communities will have a better chance of survival and improvement through their partnerships with educational institutions. Is not the final purpose of education the survival of the community, through the development of the potential of each individual?

## TEACHER VS. LEARNER RESPONSIBILITY IN MANAGEMENT EDUCATION*
J. Scott Armstrong

The goal of management education is to produce more effective managers. Whether a program initially focuses on knowledge acquisition, on attitude change, or directly upon behavioral change, the ultimate goal is behavioral change. Do graduates of an educational program perform more effectively as a result of that program?

This paper describes two basic strategies for management education. The "traditional" strategy places responsibility for education upon the teacher. An alternative strategy, called "natural learning," places responsibility upon the learner. A highly structured approach is presented for implementing natural learning. It is called SOS, for "self-oriented skill-training."

A review of the empirical literature is then presented. This compares the effectiveness of

*Reprinted with permission of the author, J. Scott Armstrong, Wharton School, University of Pennsylvania.

the traditional and SOS approaches to education. Effectiveness is judged primarily by long-term behavioral change, but other criteria are also considered.

## STRATEGIES FOR MANAGEMENT EDUCATION

People do learn. This is obvious. But do they learn more efficiently in formal educational programs than they do outside of such programs? The answer is not obvious. Furthermore, under what type of formal program would they learn most effectively? The last question is of primary interest in this paper.

One way to contrast educational strategies is in terms of responsibility. Who feels responsible for making the educational effort a success? For formal programs, it becomes a question of whether it is the teacher or the learner who is responsible.

The traditional approach to management education holds the teacher responsible for the change process. There are two key assumptions: first, that the teacher knows what is best for the learner; and, second, that the learner will change as instructed. The traditional approach is clearly the dominant one in formal education. If you are unclear about the meaning of responsibility in this context, try a simple test: remove the teacher from the classroom. Students will usually claim that they are helpless as learners in such a situation.

The traditional approach does not aim directly at behavioral change. It does not seem appropriate for a teacher to try to change the way someone acts if the behavior is important to that person. This is strongly resisted by students; it is regarded as a manipulative program. Thus, the teacher responsibility strategy limits the objectives of the program to the transmission of knowledge or "content."

Research from psychology contrasts sharply with the assumptions of the traditional roles in education. This research (e.g., see reviews by Blumberg, 1968, and by Condry, 1977) suggests that the change process is most effective when those who are changing are in control of the change process. In other words, the learner should take responsibility for change. The basic assumptions would be: (1) the learner knows what is best for him, and (2) the learner can successfully bring about change. There is no need to restrict the objectives to content because people find it acceptable to change their own behavior.

In fact, all of us have experienced responsibility for our own learning. We used it to learn such basic (and difficult) skills as speaking our native language and walking. As a result, we refer to the learner-responsible strategy as natural learning.

### The Learning Process

Most learners are unaware of the process by which they learn (Nisbett & Wilson, 1977). A better understanding of this process could lead to the development of a more efficient strategy for learning.

My review of the educational literature led to the identification of four key steps in learning. These steps are setting objectives; selecting and completing learning tasks; reviewing; and applying what was learned. The steps are illustrated in Exhibit 1, with the arrows indicating time priorities.

Exhibit 1

## KEY STEPS IN THE LEARNING PROCESS

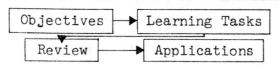

Below, SOS is contrasted with the traditional approach for each of these four steps in the learning process. As will be seen, SOS is designed to help the learner gain control over and devote energy to each step. In view of the different role of the teacher in the SOS approach, I use the term "facilitator".

### Setting Objectives

Participants in traditional education typically have ill-defined objectives. There is a way to test this: ask them. The traditional role leads the learner to claim an inability to set specific goals. Learners provide vague generalities such as "I want to learn more about management." Probing beyond this often creates stress.

The lack of responsibility for selecting learning objectives is implied by "required courses" in degree programs, and by the fact that participants in advanced management programs seldom select the program. Powell and Davis (1973) found only 6% of the participants were involved in the selection of advanced management programs.

Although teachers in traditional programs are expected to set objectives, this step seldom receives much attention. Traditional programs are typically defined in terms of inputs (learning tasks) not outputs (objectives); objectives are implicit, not explicit.

On occasion teachers do provide explicit objectives. This increased clarity of objectives would be expected to improve the learning process. Nevertheless, research on explicit objective setting by teachers ("teaching-by-

objectives") suggests that it produces only minor benefits (see the review by Duchastel and Merrill, 1973).

Although clarity of goals is desirable, an equally important aspect is the learner's commitment to objectives (e.g., Blumberg, 1968; Locke, 1968). The SOS strategy attempts to gain commitment by asking the learner to write out the objectives. These objectives should be personally meaningful. Commitment is also sought by giving the learner a high degree of choice in the selection of objectives.

It is important that SOS objectives be clearly stated and specific (e.g., see Locke, 1968).
  * Example: "I want to improve my group leadership skills."
The objectives should also be measurable (e.g., see McFall, 1970).
  * Example: "I will to master 5 new leadership skills within the next month."
In identifying measures of success, it also seems helpful to concentrate on successful changes rather than upon failures. For example, to reduce smoking, it is better to measure the number of times you wanted to smoke but did not (successes) rather than the number of cigarettes you smoked (failures).

Facilitators do not motivate the learner nor "share responsibility". They listen, suggest possible goals, and encourage the learner to find goals that are clearly stated and measurable.

### Selecting and Completing Learning Tasks

Under the traditional program, the teacher is responsible for selecting learning tasks and for designing appropriate controls to ensure that tasks are completed. The tasks focus on content and generally avoid areas that could cause conflict between the teacher and the learner. The emphasis is on having the participants perform successfully; failure is to be avoided. Teachers are generally

advised to stress positive reinforcement.

Under SOS, the learner is responsible for selecting and performing suitable tasks. The
learner develops an explicit
list of tasks, along with a plan
for how much time to spend, when
to start and when to complete
each task. According to Condry
(1977), it is important that the
learner have control over selection and performance of the
tasks.

The experiential exercise is
of particular importance in SOS.
It uses the learner's experience
as a base.

   * Example: "The learner makes
     a video tape of a meeting
     where he is the group lead-
     er."

Lewin's (1952) theory on change
is useful in designing experiential exercises. The learner
first goes through an unfreezing
process, then a change process.
A brief description of the experiential exercise is presented
in Exhibit 2. (A more detailed
description can be found in
Armstrong, 1976, and examples
are presented in Armstrong,
1977a and 1977b. Similar designs are also suggested by
Goodacre (1960) and Gibb (1958)).

## Exhibit 2
## DESIGN OF AN EXPERIENTIAL EXERCISE

---

### UNFREEZE
1 - Prior Experience Described
    by Learner
2 - Experience Generated in
    Structured Exercise
3 - Disconfirming Evidence
    Made Available

---

### CHANGE
1 - Description of Alterna-
    tive Approaches
2 - Practice New Approaches in
    Supportive Atmosphere

---

### REFREEZE
1 - Learner Writes Summary of
    Changes
2 - Learner Plans Applications

---

In contrast to the traditional
approach, which stresses positive
reinforcement, the experiential
exercise calls for negative reinforcement in the unfreezing phase
and positive reinforcement in the
changing phase. Such a strategy
is only expected to be effective
where the learner is in control of
the change process. In view of
the lack of learner control, experiential exercises would not
appear to have much value for traditional programs. In fact,
Wolfe's (1975) review of the evidence concluded that experiential
exercises were of little value.

Role playing provides a particularly valuable type of experiential exercise. It reduces the
threat in obtaining disconfirming
evidence (e.g., see Armstrong,
1976). Also, it can be used to
provide support when trying new
behavior.

   * Example: "For this meeting,
     assume that you are John
     Smith, a very effective group
     leader." (Done with a sup-
     portive group.)

Role playing seems effective for
short term changes (see review by
Kidron, 1977).

The facilitator in SOS helps by
suggesting learning tasks and by
providing descriptions of the objectives and required resources
for each task. This description
should include the time requirements for each task. The tasks
could be group or individual,

self-run or instructor-run, active or passive. Furthermore, the facilitator should try to provide an environment where participants feel free to experiment. Both the facilitator and the other participants should provide support when a learner experiments with new behavior (Scott, 1957).

In summary, SOS will open up possibilities for participants to experiment or, to "do something wrong"; the traditional program emphasizes doing things right. SOS emphasizes the willingness to change; the traditional program emphasizes the use of existing attitudes and behavior.

Reviewing Progress

Knowledge of performance is clearly important to learning (Ammons, 1956). This knowledge should go beyond "success" or "failure" to provide information on the factors related to success (Newton, 1965).

In the traditional program, the examination provides the basis for the review. Examinations are designed to see how well the learner has met the teacher's objectives, and thus create stress in learners. This stress leads to infrequent reviews; for example, reviews are usually discarded in advanced management programs.

The traditional program frequently ties in rewards (grades) with the review. According to the research on rewards (Condry, 1977; Levine and Fasnacht, 1974), extrinsic rewards increase production but they decrease learning. With rewards, learners are more answer oriented and less process oriented; they seek easier tasks; become less logical in their use of information, and reduce their creativity. Finally, extrinsic rewards seem to lessen the learner's subsequent interest in the task (Lepper, Greene and Nisbett, 1973).

Under SOS, the responsibility for the review falls upon the learner. Participation in the SOS process requires that the learner write a review after each learning task to describe success in reaching the learning objectives. (The importance of tying the review back to objectives is shown in Locke 1968.)

The philosophy behind the review is that the learner avoids evaluating things outside oneself. When one finds fault with others, or with the situation, he loses responsibility for using the situation as a learning experience. The learner should take responsibility for finding something meaningful from each task. The review contains a specific description of what was learned that was useful to the learner. The facilitator acts as a listener and encourages the learner to obtain something useful from each task. The facilitator also tries to ensure that there is no evaluation of things outside the learner; thus, there should be no learner evaluation of peers, tasks or faculty.

Applications

Learning is not complete until the learner applies what was learned. Furthermore, the extent to which the learner can generalize is of key importance: Thus, it is useful to generalize to other courses, and still more useful to practice applications on-the-job.

Traditional education typically gives no explicit consideration to the applications phase. It merely assumes that the learner will make use of what was learned.

Under SOS, the learner is asked to write plans for applications of new behavior in order to make things happen. The plan should specify the behavior (e.g., "I will use visual aids"), the situation ("in my next departmental meeting"), and the time ("by November 21"). These promises to oneself become the focal point of the formal program. With a written commitment, the likelihood of applications is high (Valiquet, 1968, presents evidence on this issue).

Learners should have confidence that they can make important changes, but they should plan for small steps. They can apply the foot-in-the-door strategy to plan a small action in the near future. This helps to keep alive the

ambitious plans for applications (Snyder and Cunningham, 1975).

## Comparing Traditional and SOS Strategies

A comparison of the traditional and SOS strategies is provided in Exhibit 3. The key points are that under SOS the learning process is explicit and the learner has control over the process.

### Exhibit 3
### COMPARISON OF TRADITIONAL AND SOS STRATEGIES

|                | Traditional             | SOS                        |
|----------------|-------------------------|----------------------------|
| Objectives     | * Set by teacher        | * Set by learner           |
|                | * Knowledge             | * Behavior                 |
|                | * Not explicit          | * Explicit                 |
| Learning Tasks | * Designed by teacher   | * Scheduled by learner     |
|                | * Required              | * Optional                 |
|                | * Emphasize success     | * Provide disconfirming evidence |
| Review         | * Directed by teacher   | * Directed by learner      |
|                | * Infrequent            | * Frequent                 |
| Applications   | * No explicit plan      | * Learner writes plan      |

## REFERENCES

Ammons, R.B., "Effects of Knowledge of Performance: A Survey and Tentative Theoretical Formulation," Journal of General Psychology, 54 (1956), 279-299.

Armstrong, J. Scott, "The Panalba Role Playing Case," in Kenneth L. Bernhardt (ed.), Marketing: 1776-1976 and Beyond. Chicago: American Marketing Association, 1976, pp. 213-216.

Armstrong, J. Scott, "Designing and Using Experiential Exercises," in M. Wayne DeLozier, et al. (eds.), Experiential Learning in Marketing Education. Columbia, S.C.:

Division of Research, College of Business Administration, University of South Carolina, 1977a, pp. 8-17.

Armstrong, J. Scott, "Forecasting the Air Travel Market," in M. Wayne DeLozier, et al. (eds.), Experiential Learning Exercises in Marketing. Santa Monica, California: Goodyear (1977b), pp. 33-47.

Blumberg, Paul, Industrial Democracy: The Sociology of Participation. New York: Schocken Books, 1968.

Condry, John, "Enemies of Exploration: Self-Initiated Versus Other-Initiated Learning," Journal of Personality and Social Psychology, 35 (1977), 459-477.

Duchastel, Phillipe C. and Merrill, P.F., "The Effects of Behavioral Objectives on Learning: A Review of Empirical Studies," Review of Educational Research, 43 (Winter 1973), 53-69.

Gibb, J.R., "A Climate for Learning," Adult Education, 9 (Autumn 1958), 19-22.

Goodacre, D.M., "Changing On-the-Job Behavior," Personnel, 37 (May-June 1960), 58-62.

Kidron, Aryeh G., "The Effectiveness of Experiential Methods in Training and Education: The Case of Role Playing," Academy of Management Review, 2 (1977), 490-495.

Lepper, M.R.; Greene, D.; and Nisbett, R.E., "Undermining Children's Intrinsic Interest with Extrinsic Rewards: A Test of the Overjustification Hypothesis," Journal of Personality and Social Psychology, 28 (1973), 129-137.

Levine, Frederic M. and Fasnacht, G., "Token Rewards May Lead to Token Learning," American Psychologist, 29 (1974), 816-820.

Lewin, Kurt, Field Theory in Social Sciences; Selected Theoretical Papers, London: Tavistock Publications, 1952.

Locke, Edwin A., "Toward a Theory of Task Motivation and Incentives," Organizational Behavior and Human Performance, 3 (1968), 157-189.

McFall, R.M., "Effects of Self-Monitoring on Normal Smoking Behavior," Journal of Consulting and Clinical Psychology, 35 (1970), 135-142.

Newton, Joseph R., "Judgment and Feedback in a Qasi-Clinical Situation," Journal of Personality and Social Psychology, 1 (1965), 336-347.

Nisbett, Richard E. and Wilson, T.D., "Telling More Than We Can Know: Verbal Reports on Mental Processes," Psychological Review, 84 (1977), 231-259.

Powell, Reed M. and Davis, Charles S., "Do University Executive Development Programs Pay Off?", Business Horizons, 16 (August 1973), 81-87.

Snyder, Mark and Cunningham, M.R., "To Comply or Not to Comply: Testing the Self-Perception Explanation of the Foot-in-the Door Phenomenon", Journal of Personality and Social Psychology, 31 (1975), 64-67.

Valiquet, M.I., "Individual Change in a Management Development Program," Journal of Applied Behavioral Science, 4 (1968), 313-325.

Wolfe, Joseph, "A Comparative Evaluation of the Experiential Approach as a Business Policy Learning Environment," Academy of Management Journal, 18 (1975), 442-452.

Part Three

## GUIDELINES FOR FIELD EXPERIENCE

> The art of teaching is the art of assisting
> discovery.
> - Mark Van Doren

### Introduction

Degree programs in the helping professions have utilized field training
components for many years.  The idea of internships was apparently brought
to the United States during the latter part of the 19th century by medical
students who had studied in Europe.  There the term "intern" had been used
to designate students who boarded at the school where they studied, as
contrasted to "externs" who studied at a school but did not board there.
Over the years the term "internship" came to mean a period of supervised
professional education designed to help a student make the difficult transition from studies in school to actual practice in a profession (Hoekstra,
1975, p. 2).

During the past twenty years, internships have become established practice for preparation in a variety of professional fields, including public
school and higher education administration, urban affairs, public administration, nursing, ministry, social work, library science, counseling, and
student affairs.  With specific reference to postsecondary education, the
mission of an internship experience is to prepare participants to become
competent professionals skilled in counseling, personnel or institutional
management, and instructional development for higher education institutions
and non-collegiate organizations.

To achieve an acceptable level of competency, participants must master
both a body of knowledge and the basic skills and techniques of the professional counselor, administrator or instructor.  Transmitting a body of
knowledge is a task that can be readily accomplished within the classroom.
However, related skills and techniques must be mastered through practice,
whether through role playing, other simulations, or actual field-based
experience.  A combination of theory and practice can be said to contribute most to optimal skill development.

The degree to which these learning objectives can be achieved is dependent upon the quality of cooperation between host institutions and the university.  An internship is never a one-way experience.  It is potentially
beneficial to the participant, the cooperating institution, and the students, employees, or clients served by that institution.  Most importantly,

73

the internship provides the opportunity for participants to test theories and personal approaches while contributing to organizational goals.

Of equal importance to the personal learning aspect of the internship is the contribution that can be made to the cooperating agency. Interns are generally considered to be fully functioning members of the institution, business, or agency's professional staff for the duration of the internship. As such, interns assist staff with normal duties, and they may increase organizational output or otherwise effect change by conducting short-term projects. As a result, the intern learns and the organization gains a part-time professional staff member.

The four chapters of Part Three identify an internship model including detailed outlines for two learning approaches. Forms and instruments related to the model are contained in the Appendix.

Chapter 4 presents an overview of the internship model, identifies the rationale for its structure and outlines basic requirements including a set of activities designed to assist the participant in assessing current knowledge and planning personal learning objectives. Chapter 5 outlines in detail the activities involved in developing and carrying out a learning contract. Similarly, Chapter 6 discusses the action research project option. Chapter 7 presents helpful guidelines for the preparation of job search materials.

Part Three concludes with two selected readings, one chosen for its careful description of journal writing techniques and the second for its presentation on resume preparation.

Chapter 4

# A MODEL FOR INTERNSHIP LEARNING IN
# POSTSECONDARY EDUCATION

> If you're not sure where you're going, any
> road looks good.
>
> - American Proverb

Listed below are ten general goals for an internship in postsecondary education. These overall goals are to be augmented by specific learning objectives to be formulated by participants in collaboration with instructors or field supervisors.

1. To provide participants an opportunity to relate coursework, research, independent study, and simulated experience to actual problems under the direction of an experienced supervisor.

2. To make participants cognizant of the responsibilities and duties of the professional personnel in their area of concentration.

3. To acquaint participants with the on-site resources available to postsecondary education instructors, counselors, administrators and others.

4. To provide opportunities for gaining experience in the processes associated with instruction, administration, or counseling in postsecondary education.

5. To make participants aware of the agencies, both complementary and competing, with which the intern's organization relates.

6. To develop skills in the task areas normally associated with the roles of administrator, counselor, or instructor.

7. To become acquainted with the laws, policies, and regulations which govern the operation of the host organization.

8. To obtain experience in working through and with others toward the realization of common objectives.

9. To become aware of sources and processes for obtaining necessary data regarding the host organization.

10. To experience the coordination of the host organization's human and material energies.

## Model for Internship Learning in Postsecondary Education

The Model for Internship Learning proposed in this text was developed and refined over several years of working with interns in a Master's degree program in postsecondary education. The model attempts to optimize the intern's ability to become a self-directed learner. At the same time, it seeks to limit unproductive learning experiences. An underlying assumption is that the intern must assume personal responsibility for learning if the internship is to achieve its potential value for the individuals and for the organizations involved. The model (see Figure 2) represents a framework in which self-directed learning can be fostered.

Background and Pre-assessment: At this early point in the internship, prospective interns are called upon to assess their prior learning and professional competence. Persons approaching the process of internship planning typically bring with them some background in professional experience and/or course work. What has already been learned experientially need not be repeated unless the learner's objective is to strengthen existing skills. Before practical activities can be devised, participants must decide upon which of two major learning options they prefer in carrying out the internship - the Learning Contract or the Learning Project.

Practical Activities: The first option, shown at the top of Figure 2, calls upon the participant to devise a learning contract consisting of a variety of learning experiences. Additionally, participants may engage in several explorations of specific issues or problems and visit outside the internship site to assess the solutions which others have applied to problems. The second option, an Action Research Project, is shown in the lower part of Figure 2. Participants whose careers in postsecondary education are already established often choose this mode for internship participation. The project option calls upon the intern to conduct an in-depth study of a single problem while ultimately carrying the project through to completion within the organization.

Analysis/Evaluation: Analysis and evaluation of learning are among the most important of internship activities. Accordingly, Chapter 8 in Part Four is devoted solely to evaluation procedures. Evaluation serves the basic function of assessing learning that has occurred but, of course, evaluation is a learning experience in itself. Participants electing to pursue a learning contract are advised to prepare a Log of Experience which has as its objective the relating of theory with practice. Additionally, learning is possible through observation and exploration activities. Participants electing the project option engage in self-evaluation while eliciting evaluation from supervisors and others.

Career Application: Finally, the Model for Internship Learning provides an opportunity for students to prepare professional credentials. Chapter 7 provides guidelines and examples.

## Specific Internship Requirements

In order to accomplish the objectives of the internship, participants should consider completion of the following activities:

# Figure 2. Postsecondary Education Internship: Overview

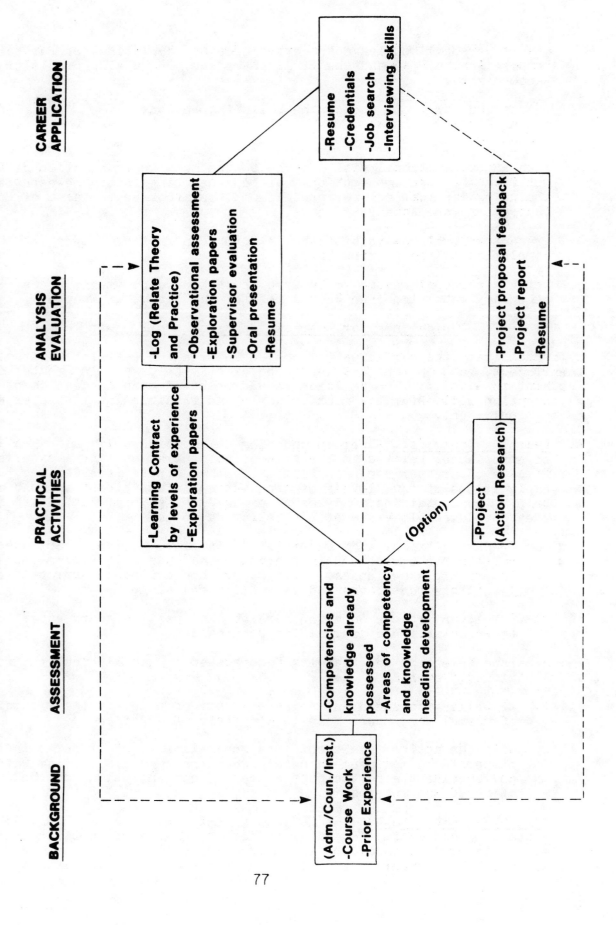

77

1. Assess personal knowledge and experience by completing the Participant Résumé (Appendix A) and the Preliminary Learning Goals Formulator (Appendix B).

2. Select and carry out one of the following options:
   a. A Learning Contract.
   b. An Action Research Project.

3. Make an observational visit to one postsecondary organization different from the host institution. Write a description of the experience including implications for professional behavior in the area of concentration (see Appendix J).

4. Present an oral analysis of the Learning Contract or Project at the completion of the Internship.

5. Write a personal résumé to be used in seeking employment in postsecondary education (see Guidelines for the Résumé in Chapter 7).

### Guidelines for Learning Contract and Project

To facilitate the participants' choice between the Learning Contract and the Project, both options are described briefly below and in greater detail in Chapters 5 and 6. The decision should be based upon an assessment as to which option will offer the most valuable and feasible Internship experience to the individual.

A. Learning Contract. A person choosing this option will gain a variety of experiences related to the area of concentration. Some experiences will be of greater depth and intensity than others (see Chapter 5 for explanations of four levels of experience). Participants should maintain a Log containing analyses of experiences gained. In addition, they should complete one of the following options:

   1. Prepare 3 Exploration Papers each discussing a significant question relating to postsecondary education that has arisen from the internship experiences. Each paper should include appropriate literature references and personal conclusions.

   2. Submit an article on a topic related to postsecondary education to an established journal for publication.

A person selecting the Learning Contract option should meet the following requirements:

   1. Be willing to spend an adequate amount of time within or outside of normal work hours to gain a variety of experiences.

   2. Gain the active commitment of a supervisor or other person(s) to cooperate in making meaningful experiences available from within and outside the participant's area of concentration for the duration of the internship.

B. Action Research Project. This option centers in the planning, implementation, and evaluation of a project in an area of specific interest. The project should be in an area where the participant is not already highly experienced. The participant will be involved as the facilitator of an action research project designed to strengthen or improve educational practice within the organization. The person choosing this option will prepare a written proposal (planning document) at the outset and a written evaluation of the project at its conclusion.

A person selecting this option should meet the following requirements:

1. Be committed to the achievement of the project objectives.

2. Gain the approval and appropriate cooperation of a supervisor and other relevant persons in the design and implementation of the project.

### Role of Internship Instructor

The instructor will consult with the participant throughout the internship regarding progress on the Learning Contract or Project. In addition, the instructor should maintain periodic contact with the participant's field supervisor(s).

### Pre-Assessment and Learning Needs

The selection and design of learning activities are always best approached through clearly established goals. This is particularly true for the experiential mode of learning. Random experiences produce random learning. Goal setting must, therefore, precede the development of either a Learning Contract or Action Research Project.

This section identifies three tools useful in assessing the nature of prior experience and formal learning. A Participant Résumé (Appendix A) listing prior job and educational activities is designed to assist the intern in recalling all related learning while identifying immediate career goals. The Preliminary Learning Goals Formulator (Appendix B) poses a series of questions designed to identify the intern's areas of functional strength and weakness related to career goals. Finally, the Learning Goals Self-Evaluation Form (Appendix C) requires that specific learning objectives be formulated.

The importance of these preliminary assessment activities cannot be overstated. Participants are encouraged to carefully review the outcomes of self-assessment with their internship instructor before proceeding with planning either a Learning Contract or Action Research Project.

Chapter 5

## THE LEARNING CONTRACT

> I hear and I forget.  I see and I remember.
> I do and I understand.
>
> - Chinese Proverb

Having completed the processes of self-assessment and setting personal learning objectives, the participant is ready to use these objectives in forming a Learning Contract.  This chapter is a guide in that activity. It contains definitions of levels of experience and requirements for the Learning Contract, suggested activities, and guidelines for the Learning Experience Log and Exploration Papers.  The final section identifies suggested guidelines for organizational visitations.  Chapter 6 provides information for participants who elect to conduct an Action Research Project.

### Definitions of Levels of Experience and Requirements for the Learning Contract

A.  DEFINITIONS

### Level 1 Experience:  Observation

The intern is present while relevant organizational activities are being carried out.  The intern is free to observe, but does not participate in a significant way.  Examples might include:  visiting an administrative council session; attending an academic department meeting; watching a counselor working with a client.

### Level 2 Experience:  Interview or Discussion

The intern conducts an in-depth discussion with one or more persons regarding particular areas of administrative, instructional, or counseling theory or action.  Examples might include:  interviewing a department head for ideas regarding staff development; discussing with a manager methods of allocating funds; interviewing several counselors regarding ways of assisting students who are returning to education after a long absence.

Level 3 Experience:  Limited Participation

The intern performs short term professional activities in order
to become familiar with new areas.  Examples might include:
talking with students who have admission deficiencies and recommending actions which might be taken; preparing recommendations
for a proposed position; addressing a meeting on a selected
topic; completing physical arrangements for an institute or
conference.

Level 4 Experience:  Sustained Participation

The intern assumes responsibility for the planning, implementation, and evaluation of on-going projects.  Examples might include:  assuming the chairmanship of a curriculum development
committee; developing and field-testing a system of instructional
evaluation; planning a departmental or institutional budget for
the coming year.

B.  REQUIREMENTS

During the course of the Internship Learning Contract, the following minimum requirements are suggested:

1.  At least two Level 4 experiences should be attained.

2.  At least six Level 3 experiences should be attained.

3.  At least ten Level 1 or 2 experiences should be attained.

It might be possible for higher level experiences to take the
place of lower level experiences.  Such arrangements should be
determined in consultation with the internship instructor and
field supervisor.

### Suggested Activities for the Three Areas of Concentration

   Listed below are suggestions for activities in three areas of concentration:  Instruction, Administration, and Counseling.  They are not meant to
be all inclusive or prescriptive but are intended to stimulate thinking.
The coding (1, 2, 3, 4) corresponds to the levels of experience described
above.

A.  Instruction

Level
   1.   Observe the work of other instructors or trainers to
        identify alternative instructional approaches.  (Ob-
        servation might be focused outside one's area of con-
        centration.)

   2.   Interview department heads, coordinators, directors,
        or deans relative to the major curricular and instruc-
        tional problems they face and discuss possible avenues
        toward solution.

3. Establish a discussion group to deal with special topics and concerns of the staff.

   Develop a plan for appraising instructional effectiveness.

   Develop a plan for communicating (sharing) new instructional ideas, materials, methodologies.

   Write a proposal for foundation or institutional funding to develop a new program or to modify an existing program.

   Assess the degree of integration of federal programs within the institution's instructional framework.

4. Plan and implement development programs for the instructional staff.

   Plan and implement a curriculum development committee that is responsible for major revisions, evaluations, or developments in instructional programs.

   Chair a curriculum committee.

   Plan and implement a program assessment effort in one instructional/training area.

   Become knowledgeable of and assess the use of available instructional materials and develop and implement a plan for improving upon present usage.

   Develop a set of instructional/learning materials that will facilitate the delivery of a specific content area within program or curriculum.

B. Administration

Level
1. Observe the operation and effectiveness of student affairs offices.

   Observe administrative styles of staff interaction.

   Observe administrator strategies for working with community and professional groups.

   Study the various budgetary and financial forms and reports that are utilized by specific offices or divisions of an institution.

2. Discuss with administrative staff alternative plans for coping with problems identified by students through student government organizations.

   Interview department heads or deans relative to the procedures followed in documenting personnel ineffectiveness.

Interview board members or other members of the community relative to the purpose of the institution.

Interview the comptroller or member of his/her staff to determine what problems ensue from trying to assure effective service.

3. Review the institution's dismissal procedures to assure incorporation of due process.

   Analyze accounting and record keeping procedures and write an assessment report.

   Identify the areas of need for student/employee development programming.

   Review personnel policies and make recommendations for change.

   Plan an orientation and training session for new staff persons.

   Analyze the community's power structure and its effect upon the institution.

   Prepare a staff work schedule, reporting form, or other document related to work flow.

   Develop a process for assessing the physical needs of the office, division, department, or institution.

   Write specifications for equipment needs in a building or specific work or instructional area.

   Analyze the food service program and formulate a plan for maximum efficiency.

   Participate in the planning for a redesign of existing facilities.

   Prepare a budget for program, department, or other institutional unit.

4. Design and implement, in cooperation with administrative staff, a plan for increasing enrollments, or delivering increased program information to the community, or increasing the effectiveness of first line communicators in the institution.

   Plan and implement a series of staff development programs which offer promise of meeting the needs of instructional and administrative staff in the organization.

   Develop and implement a plan or strategy for appraising staff effectiveness.

Design and implement a community survey on attitudes toward the institution.

Plan and provide leadership for a program designed to inform the community of an instructional program.

Plan and implement a community education program.

Develop, in cooperation with administrators, a control system for requisitions, purchase orders, and goods received.

Develop a program to identify alumni as contributors to institutional development.

C.  Counseling

Level
1.  Observe the daily routine of the office or agency and catalogue the activities and roles of various persons.

Observe a group guidance activity (information giving, decision-making, orientation, etc.).

Observe an initial or intake counseling session for individual counseling.

Observe an intake interview for group counseling.

Observe an individual counseling session.

Observe a group counseling session.

2.  Interview a counselor about his/her role and functions in the office or agency.

Discuss the planning, goals, and expected outcomes for a group guidance activity to be conducted by a counselor.

Interview a key clerical staff person about his/her responsibilities.

Interview a counselor about a counseling session you have observed to learn how your perceptions relate to those of the counselor.

3.  Meet with incoming students to familiarize them with the counseling office and help them get to the appropriate source of help.

Administer tests or instruments under the guidance of experienced personnel.

Engage in information dispensing helping activities.

Plan and conduct a group guidance activity.

4. Plan and implement a community outreach program.

   Co-lead a series of counseling or growth groups.

   Conduct individual counseling if adequate on-site supervision is provided.

### Guidelines for Learning Experience Log and Exploration Papers

In order to assist in the organization and documentation of the variety of learning experiences gained during the Learning Contract, the following guidelines for the Learning Experience Log and Exploration Papers are presented.

A. Organization of the Learning Experience Log

   Set up a three-ring loose leaf notebook for 8-1/2" x 11" paper and four tabs as follows:

   1. Level 1 Experiences - Observation
   2. Level 2 Experiences - Interview or Discussion
   3. Level 3 Experiences - Limited Participation
   4. Level 4 Experiences - Sustained Participation

   As experiences are gained at the various levels, keep a record of them in the appropriate sections of the Learning Experience Log.

B. Recording Experiences

   1. Level 3 and Level 4 Experiences

      For each Level 3 and Level 4 experience, complete a Learning Experience Overview Log Sheet (Appendix D) at the inception of the project or activity. This is a planning guide for each experience. As each Level 3 or 4 experience develops, use the Log Entry Form (Appendix E) to record progress toward the objectives. The purpose of the Log Entry Form is to document learning on an on-going basis. It can be thought of as a learning diary or journal.

      It is recommended that a Log Entry Form be completed for each Level 3 and 4 experience at least once a week. In this way, maximum learning from experience may be captured for further reference and study. Materials, such as memos, brief reports, instruments, or other items prepared by the intern may be attached to Log Entry Forms when appropriate.

   2. Level 1 and Level 2 Experiences

      Since at Level 1 and 2 each learning experience will probably occur in one session, a Log Entry Form (Appendix E) should be completed at the conclusion of each experience. Observations or discussions which are integral parts of Level 3 and 4 experiences should be recorded as parts of those experiences. In filling out Log Entry Forms for Level 1 and 2 experiences, strive for depth of analysis in order to gain as much insight as possible.

3. Focus on Learning from Experience

The major purpose of the Learning Experience Log is not to
merely describe the experiences gained but to encourage
reflection upon the meaning of those experiences in the
light of career goals. Therefore, it is suggested that
the Summary of Experiences sections of the Log Entry Forms
be kept rather brief and the Analysis sections be written
as candidly and completely as possible. Feelings, concepts and generalizations related to the experiences,
theoretical considerations, and questions that require
further investigation should be included. Refer to the
Selected Reading by Daly (page 105) for further suggestions about the use of learning journals.

C. Writing the Exploration Papers

If the Learning Contract option is selected, three papers should be
submitted during the internship. Each paper should explore a significant question or topic relating to postsecondary education that
arose during the internship experiences.

Entries in the Log Entry Forms under "Questions or Topics Needing
Further Investigation" provide raw data from which significant
questions or topics may be chosen.

Each Exploration Paper should include the following:

1. A clear statement of the question or topic to be explored.

2. A brief description of the experience(s) that raised this
   question or topic.

3. A brief review of further interviews and pertinent theoretical and/or research literature bearing on the question or
   topic. (Appropriate footnotes and bibliography should be
   included.)

4. Personal thoughts and conclusions regarding the question
   or topic under discussion.

### Guidelines for Organizational Visitations

An organizational visitation is suggested for every intern whether the
Learning Contract or the Action Research Project is selected.

1. Visitations are to be made in departments, divisions, or offices at
   institutions other than the intern's host site.

2. The intern should have specific objectives for the visitation before
   going.

3. The objectives should be directed toward the intern's learning
   experiences.

4. The length of time for the visitation should be sufficient to
   achieve the specific visitation objective.

5. After each visitation, the intern should (a) summarize the experiences; (b) relate any ideas gained that might be useful for his own field experiences; (c) ask questions that might be further explored.

6. A recommended format for reporting the visitation is located in Appendix J.

Chapter 6

## THE LEARNING PROJECT

> You can teach a student a lesson for a day;
> but if you can teach him to learn by creat-
> ing curiosity, he will continue the learning
> process as long as he lives.
>
> Clay P. Bedford

This chapter is designed to assist in the development of an Action
Research Project. As with the Learning Contract, it is essential that
the self-assessment and learning objectives materials identified in Chapter 4 be completed. The Project is referred to as an action research
project rather than a formal educational research project because internships, even when research-oriented, usually focus primarily upon applied
problems. For help in making the distinction between formal and action
research, refer to Figure 3. The final section of this chapter lists
Guidelines for Preparing the Final Project Report. The Final Project
Report will serve its major function as an evaluation document. Additional forms which can be used for feedback and evaluation of both the
Project Proposal and Final Report are found in Appendix H and I.

### An Approach to Project Design

In order to assist in the orderly and logical development of the Learning Project, the components of project design are outlined below. Each
of the nine components is briefly defined, and a series of questions is
provided for each component as a guide to project development.

The final written Project Proposal should contain nine sections (one
section for each component), with each section of sufficient length to
adequately describe thoughts and plans in the particular area. If particular questions within any of the sections do not apply to the Project
in mind, revise the questions or add more appropriate ones.

A. Statement of the Project Goal

   This section presents a concise explanation of what you are attempt-
   ing to accomplish in the project:

   1. In what area of concentration will your project be carried out?

Figure 3.  SOME DIFFERENCES BETWEEN FORMAL EDUCATIONAL
RESEARCH AND ACTION RESEARCH[1]

| | Areas | Formal Research | Action Research |
|---|---|---|---|
| 1. | Training Required | Extensive training in measurement, statistics, and research methods. | Limited training needed because of less rigorous design. |
| 2. | Goals | To obtain widely generalizable knowledge. | To obtain knowledge that can be applied directly to local situations. |
| 3. | Hypotheses/ Objectives | Highly specific hypotheses that are testable. | Specific hypotheses or objectives that can be measured. |
| 4. | Review of Literature | Extensive review of primary source material. | Review of available primary & secondary sources. |
| 5. | Sampling | Random or unbiased sample from population is sought. | Individuals and groups available to researcher are used as subjects. |
| 6. | Experimental Design | Careful design to reduce error and control extraneous variable. | Procedures are planned, but changes can be made as needed during project. |
| 7. | Measurement | The most valid and reliable measurement tools are employed. | Less rigorous standards regarding measurement tools employed. |
| 8. | Analysis of Data | Complex analysis with emphasis on statistical significance. | Practical, rather than statistical, significance is emphasized. |
| 9. | Application of Results | Able to be applied over a large area of theory and practice. | Applied immediately to primarily local situations. |

[1] Adapted from EDUCATIONAL RESEARCH: AN INTRODUCTION, First Edition, by Walter R. Borg. Copyright © 1963 by Longman Inc. Reprinted with permission of Longman Inc., New York.

2. What general result(s) do you hope to bring about through your project (i.e., what do you hope to initiate, change, improve, determine, etc.)?

B. Background and Significance of the Project

This section contains a description of the historical setting of the project and an explanation of how the successful completion of the project will improve educational theory or practice.

1. What problems or conditions led to the selection of this project?

2. What is the setting within which this project will be carried out?

3. What effects will the successful accomplishment of this project have on educational practice?

4. How widespread are the effects of this project likely to be (i.e., a department? an organization? a system? statewide?)?

C. Specific Project Objectives

Objectives are statements of the results that the project is designed to achieve.

1. What are the specific results that the project is designed to achieve?

2. Is each specific objective measurable (i.e., is it stated in such a way that its achievement can be clearly demonstrated to someone who may be skeptical)?

3. Is each specific objective stated separately?

D. Definitions, Assumptions, Delimitations

Definitions are statements of the meanings of key terms as they are being used in the project objectives.

1. What is the definition of each key term in the Project Statement and Objectives sections?

Assumptions are factors related to the project that are not under investigation or that cannot be controlled.

1. What factors relating to people, places, and things in the project are assumed without having to check them?

Delimitations refer to areas that a project such as the present one might logically deal with but which, for one reason or another, have been placed outside the scope of this project.

1. What areas which might be a part of this project have you placed outside its scope? Explain why.

E. Review of Literature

In this section, present an examination of resources related to the project topic and a written description of the most pertinent ideas, theories, and research, with appropriate citations.

1. What other projects and studies similar to the present one have been carried out? With what results?

2. What ideas are there in the literature that are helpful in planning this project?

3. What persons might be interviewed to provide additional ideas and suggestions for the project? (Report the interview results.)

F. Project Procedures

The purpose of this section is to formulate a detailed description of the plan for carrying out the project, including who is to be involved, how they will be selected, what procedures will be carried out, what data will be collected, what measuring instruments or data-gathering techniques will be used, and how each of the specific project objectives will be evaluated.

1. What person(s) or group(s) will be involved in the project?

2. By what procedures will they be selected?

3. In a logical order, what procedures will be carried out during the project (include what kinds of data will be collected and what measuring instruments or data collecting techniques will be used)?

4. How will each specific project objective stated in Section C be measured and evaluated? Include a separate discussion of the measurement of each specific objective.

G. Project Time Schedule

This section contains a chronological listing of the project procedures with the projected date of completion for each.

1. In what order will the project procedures be carried out?

2. What is the projected completion date for each procedure?

H. Bibliography

Present a listing of all the resources used in the planning of the project.

I. Appendix

This section contains copies of materials to be used for data collection or other purposes during the course of the project. Materials may include copies of letters to be sent, forms to be completed, schedules to be used, questionnaires to be filled out, or other materials to be employed during the project.

# Guidelines for Preparing the Final Project Report

The Final Project Report is, in a sense, a continuation of the Proposal in that it incorporates the project's results. The Final Project Report should contain three major sections. Each section should be of sufficient length to adequately present results and ideas. Each of the sections of the Final Project Report is briefly defined below, and guidelines are provided to help in organizing the report. A section entitled "Attachments" may be added, if necessary, for the presentation of tables, charts, or graphs that do not fit conveniently into the text of the Report.

J. **Project Goal and Actual Procedures**

This section presents a concise explanation of what was to be accomplished in the project, and a summary, in chronological order, of the procedures actually used, with emphasis on additional and revised procedures. (Refer to Sections A and F of the Proposal in preparing this section.)

1. State the general results you hoped to achieve through your project (i.e., what you hoped to initiate, change, improve, determine, etc.).

2. In a logical order, discuss the procedures that were actually utilized during the project (include persons or groups involved, activities engaged in, kinds of data collected, and methods of data collection).

3. Include procedures which had to be revised, omitted, or added during the course of the project. Explain in each case.

K. **Project Results**

Present, interpret, and discuss the data collected during the project with special reference to the relationship of the data to each of the specific project objectives.

1. For each of the specific project objectives (refer to Section C of the Proposal) present the data which were collected. For each objective, summarize the data in narrative form, discuss the interpretation of the data, and indicate the degree to which the data support the objective. (More complete presentations of data, if appropriate, should be included in tabular or graphic form in the Attachments section.)

2. For each objective, discuss the limitations, if any, on interpreting the data. (Be sure to report adverse as well as supportive findings for each objective.)

3. Summarize the results of the overall project (take into account the data presented for all of the objectives).

L. **Conclusions and Recommendations**

Present an analysis of what has been learned in the project and a discussion of how such learning might be applied in the particular project environment and in related areas.

1. What conclusions or generalizations can be drawn from the findings of this project? (Refer to data to support conclusions.)

2. Discuss areas of the project, if any, which require further investigation.

3. Describe the modifications, if any, which might make the project more effective if it were to be repeated.

4. Describe the follow-up actions that are planned or that would be appropriate for this project.

5. What are the implications of this project? What are some related areas of practice to which the findings of this project might be applied?

M. Attachments

This section contains additional data and materials which support project conclusions but which do not fit conveniently into the text.

1. Include more complete lists of data, charts, graphs, tables, etc. which are referred to or summarized in the text.

2. Include pictures, diagrams, or other materials which document the project implementation.

Chapter 7

PREPARING TO FIND A POSITION

> To avoid criticism - Do Nothing; Say Nothing;
> Be Nothing.
>
> - Elbert Hubbard

This final chapter in Part Three was prepared to assist interns in pursuing career goals. Sections included are Guidelines for Preparation of Personal Information, Suggestions for Vita (Résumé) Writing, and three sample résumés. The Readings Section, following Chapter 7, includes an article by Frank Braun on Résumé preparation which offers additional assistance.

## Guidelines for Preparation of Personal Information

Each participant, toward the end of the internship, should have accumulated a supply of personal information that can be presented to the prospective employer during an interview or mailed prior to the interview. This job portfolio might include personal background information and describe activities in which the intern engaged. At minimum, the portfolio should include a Vita and a brief record of the internship experience.

Personal information consists of four components:

A. Vita (or Résumé)
B. Record of Internship Experience
C. Description of Related Experiences
D. Additional Supporting Materials

A. ## Vita

The Vita is a means of introducing the candidate to the employment officer before a position application is completed. As such, it is basically a sales document. It is hoped that the information on the Vita will interest the employer to the extent that the candidate will be invited to complete an application form and come for an interview.

Examine the Vita formats on pages 99 to 104. As there are various ways of presenting material in a Vita, these formats are suggestions only.

95

B.   Record of Internship Experience

The Record is a supporting document to the Vita.  Its main objectives
are to point out to the prospective employer that the intern has had
postsecondary experience and to briefly describe such experience.
Except in special cases, it should not be sent with the Vita but
reserved for use during the interview or in follow-up correspondence.

The Record should be no longer than one page, single spaced.  It
should briefly describe the kind of organization in which the internship experiences were gained, and it should describe the nature of
those experiences.  The Record of Internship Experiences may become
part of the credentials package which is sent upon request to prospective employers.  As the internship may be the only experience
that the candidate has had in postsecondary education, it is important that the description be well written.

C.   Description of Related Experiences

The purpose of this Description is to provide a summary of additional
activities in which the candidate has participated that are relevant
to positions in postsecondary education.  The Description should include those areas of service in which the candidate assumed responsibility or served in a leadership capacity.  For each activity,
briefly describe the nature of the activity, the candidate's role,
and the outcome or results achieved.  This Description of Related
Experiences may also be included as part of the credentials package.

Below is a sample system for categorizing activities in which a candidate may have participated that are relevant to a postsecondary
education role.

- Nature of Activity or Work
  Under this category, the candidate should briefly describe the
  assignment or the type of activity or work.

- Candidate's Role
  This should include the exact nature of the candidate's involvement in the activities described.  The number of people involved
  as well as the degree of the candidate's authority and responsibility should be included.

- Conclusion
  If the assignment produced an outcome that was or will be acted
  upon by the organization, this information should be included.

D.   Additional Supporting Materials

These materials should be kept for use during job interviews or when
additional information is requested by a prospective employer.
Materials in this category supplement and support information sup-
plied under categories A, B, and C above.

Examples of additional supporting materials are:  copies of published
or unpublished articles or reports, internship project papers, copies
of grant proposals, major research papers and letters of appreciation for public service.  Other materials may be appropriate as well.

# Tips for Vita (Résumé) Writing for the Postsecondary Education Candidate

## Purpose

The Vita, or Résumé, is a creative professional document designed to describe the candidate's experience to best advantage. It should be focused toward the field the candidate wants to enter. The Vita will not assure employment; its purpose is to help obtain an interview. Therefore, the Vita should answer three basic questions: where you can be reached - name, address, and phone; what you want to do - a concise statement of vocational objectives; and where you have been in terms of experience and education. The Vita is a promotional piece about you as a candidate.

## General Rules

1. Make your Vita attractive in appearance and easy to read. Group information in logically organized sections leaving ample white space on the page. The résumé should be printed or photostated - never use carbon copies. Correct all grammatical errors. Do not use sentence structure or personal pronouns - use action-packed phrases.

2. Your Vita should be brief, clear, and concise. A two-page document at most is usually sufficient. This space limitation will help you select and limit your material. When in doubt, leave it out, or seek counsel.

3. Include a generally stated job objective or statement of your vocational goal.

## Format

There are two basic styles of Vita writing:

1. Chronological or general - each job or educational experience is listed separately working back from the most recent job. Under each, list the functions that were performed. The chronological résumé format is used most frequently by people with uninterrupted work experience, usually in the field where they are seeking employment.

2. Functional - experience and training are grouped and described as functions or areas of competence, listing skills and accomplishments that relate to the job for which you are applying. This format is excellent for career changes or people with significant unpaid experience.

A combination of both approaches is often effective for it expresses chronological events in a descriptive manner. Several examples of Vitae are found on the next few pages.

## Items to Omit

1. Salary data.

2. Personal information such as age, marital status, height, weight. Let the prospective employer consider you solely on the basis of your qualifications.

## Cover Letter

A Vita should never be mailed without a cover letter. This letter should highlight certain qualifications you may have for this specific job or stress why you are interested in the particular institution or position. Make sure your closing is not vague, but states a specific next step, such as, "I'll call you in a few days to see if we can set up an appointment."

OBJECTIVE: PERSONNEL TRAINING AND DEVELOPMENT, where experience in creating innovative training programs, ability to communicate ideas effectively, and success in motivating people, will contribute to profit through planned increase of personnel productivity.

BACKGROUND SUMMARY: Twelve years of communications-oriented experience includes: Personnel Training, Leadership and Consulting; Sales and Marketing; Teaching; Program Development and Implementation.

EDUCATION: Ed.D., New York University (Adult and Higher Education). MBA, Suffolk University (Evening Division). BA, San Francisco State University (English).

RELATED ACCOMPLISHMENTS

Training and Motivating: Saved $55,000 annually in salaries of new personnel by motivating department heads in modern employee development methods. Program now in third year.

Successful in persuading members of faculty and administration to participate in school's new environmental program.

Innovative Programs: Convinced management to triple size of employee development program by demonstrating its direct contribution to company profits, with minimum investment, using present staff.

Created and implemented unique environmental program using school's own resources.

Communicating Ideas: Generated 40% sales increase within 3 months and improved employees' morale by using graphic displays to initiate incentive system.

Wrote and published article on innovative History teaching method, resulting in over 30 requests for reprints to date.

EMPLOYMENT HISTORY: Consultant. Hobart Brown Associates, Salem, New Jersey. Responsible for development of training materials, including manuals and visual aids. Set up and conducted over 50 training seminars. (1971 - present)

Manufacturer's Representative. (Self-employed). Product lines: College insignia, trophies and school furniture. Trained and motivated staff of eight successful salesmen. Personally handled all marketing and business development efforts. (1966 - 1971)

<u>Teacher</u>.  Plum Hill School, Plum Hill, New Jersey.
Responsible for curriculum development and teaching
of History.  Developed first environmental program
in school's history.  (1962 - 1966)

```
                              Your Name
                              Your Street Address
                              Your City, State & Zip Code
                              Area Code/Phone Number
```

OBJECTIVE:    Responsible Human Resource Development position allowing
              for utilization of my communications and organizational
              skills to attain increased productivity for my employer
              and myself; a position in which self-development and
              advancement will be the natural by-product of my leader-
              ship and hard work.

BACKGROUND    6 years of communications-oriented experience have includ-
SUMMARY:      ed teaching, leadership and consulting, group work, per-
              sonnel training, counseling, administration, program
              development and implementation.

EDUCATION:    Ph.D. (Higher Education), University of Michigan.
              M.Ed. (Adult Education), Boston University.
              B.A. (English), Miami University, Ohio.

RELATED ACCOMPLISHMENTS

Effective         Convinced management to triple staff through clarifica-
Communication:    tion and validation of specific task areas for office
                  management.

                  Facilitated easing of volatile situation involving manage-
                  ment and personnel allowing for greater consolidation of
                  individual efforts.

                  Bridged credibility gap between inner-office staffs
                  through breakdown of psychological barriers acting as
                  deterrent to group efforts.

Responsible       Progressed from Counselor to Director of $40,000 per year
Organization:     program providing elementary through graduate level in-
                  struction for 2,000 overseas personnel and dependents.

                  Tripled enrollment in University of Maryland Overseas
                  Program resulting in 250% increase in gross income within
                  10 months.

                  Marketed and administered 3 graduate programs totalling
                  $90,000 in annual revenue for Boston University Overseas
                  Program (Germany).

EMPLOYMENT        Education Services Specialist. General Education Develop-
HISTORY:          ment Agency, Frankfurt, Germany. Assured Education Pro-
                  gram was planned effectively and maintained within limits
                  of sound management standards. Supervised 14 people.
                  Provided counseling of students to aid in obtaining sound,
                  realistic educational/vocational objectives. Functioned
                  as consultant to Battalion and Company Commanders in the
                  areas of educational needs and drug abuse. (74 - 77)

EMPLOYMENT
HISTORY:
(cont'd)

Teaching Assistant. Boston University, Frankfurt, Germany. Supervised 10-20 graduate students involved in clinical setting. Consultative responsibilities to Professor of Psychology as well as community psychiatrist and psychologist. (73 - 74)

Administrative Assistant. Boston University, Frankfurt, Germany. Marketed and administered 3 graduate programs. Developed "on-going" relationships with students to insure effective teacher-student communications. Counseled students regards salability of degree; evaluated transcripts and worked in close proximity with Professor of Counseling Psychology.

```
                    Your Name
                    Your Street Address
                    Your City, State & Zip Code
                    Area Code/Phone Number
```

PROFESSIONAL   A career Development position working with college stu-
OBJECTIVE      dents in a Career Development Service - Placement and/or
               Counseling.

EDUCATION      M.S. Indiana University, Bloomington, Indiana (1978)
                 College Student Personnel Administration, Counseling

               B.A. Case Western Reserve University, Cleveland, Ohio (1974)
                 Psychology, Education (cum laude)

PROFESSIONAL   <u>Career Counselor Intern</u>, Salem College (West Virginia), 1978.
EXPERIENCE         Responsible for organization, development, and operation
               of the College Placement Service; Organization, operation,
               and supervision of the Career Information Center; Respon-
               sible for a variety of Outreach Programs concerning Career
               Planning and Placement.

               <u>Resident Assistant</u>, Indiana University, 1974-75.
               Responsibilities for 100 women included the creation of a
               living environment conducive to the emotional, intellec-
               tual, and social development of students; career and per-
               sonal counseling, academic advising and administration of
               discipline.
              . Organized and supervised the operation of a Career
               Resource Center in the residence center which provided
               career counseling and functioned as a liaison between
               students in the center and the various campus career
               services.
              . Designed and conducted a Career/Decision Making Workshop
               for students.
              . Served on Residence Life Staff Recruitment Steering Com-
               mittee; participated in Evaluation of entire staff
               selection process.
              . Organized and implemented staff selection process in
               residence center of 1200 students.

               <u>Practicum in the Office of Continuing Education for Women</u>
               Indiana University, Fall 1975.
               Concentrated experience in the area of Career Development
               for Adult Women.  Assisted in conducting Educational/
               Career Decision-Making Workshops for Women.  Sessions
               included:
              . Administration and interpretation of Holland's Self-
               directed Search.
              . Interpretation of Strong-Campbell Interest Inventory
               and Edwards Personal Preference Schedule.
              . Possible employment options for participants.

               Assisted in designing and conducting a Career Explora-
               tion Workshop for women which provided an opportunity
               for them to explore the world of work.

| | |
|---|---|
| PROFESSIONAL EXPERIENCE (cont.) | <u>Practicum in the Office of Educational Student Services</u> Indiana University, Spring 1975. |

Studied 5 areas of student services including Graduate School Admissions, Academic Advising, Teacher Certification, Data Processing and Records, and Placement.  Concentrated experience in the Placement Office observing counseling interviews which discussed the job search process.

**HONORS**

. Mortar Board (National Senior Honorary), Secretary 1973-4.
. Pi Lambda Theta (National Education Honorary)
. Psi Chi (National Psychology Honorary)
. National Science Foundation Program in Computer Programming held at Ohio University (Athens) during Summer 1969.
. High School representative to Library Workshop held at Kutztown State College (Pennsylvania), Spring 1969.

**PROFESSIONAL AFFILIATIONS**

American College Personnel Association
American Personnel and Guidance Association
National Association of Women Deans, Administrators and Counselors

**PREVIOUS EMPLOYMENT**

Resident Tutor in the Cleveland Public Schools (1971-1974).
Teacher in Religious School, Cleveland, Ohio (1970-1974).

Summer 1975

Kelly Girl, Inc., Cleveland, Ohio; Switchboard Operator, Medical Secretary, Legal Secretary.

1974

Tele-Video Industries, Inc., Cleveland, Ohio; Field Manager - Responsible for training and fielding company sales representatives.

1971, 1972

Vanguard Diversified, Inc., Brooklyn, New York (mfr. business furniture); Payroll Clerk, Customer Service, Computer Programming.

1970

Deborah Hospital, Brown Mills, New Jersey, Medical Secretary.

**INTERESTS**

Enjoy:  Reading, Traveling, Music, Theater, Sports, Gourmet Cooking.

**REFERENCES**

Credentials will be furnished upon request from the:

Bureau of Educational Placement
Indiana University
Bloomington, Indiana  47401

File Number 0000

## Selected Readings

USING STUDENT JOURNALS TO
INDIVIDUALIZE INSTRUCTION*
Elizabeth A. Daly

A student log used in conjunc-
tion with a practical experience
is an effective means of individualizing and personalizing instruction and learning. Essentially, a
log is a personal record of meaningful observations and reactions
written while the writer is engaged
in an in-depth practical experience.

Practicums or internships within
a particular field of activity are
often used as final transition experience designed to bridge the gap
between academic classroom study
and the real world. In the classroom, students tend to be exposed
to the history, sociology, philosophy, and contemporary theory concerning a particular field of endeavor. When the student has control over this body of knowledge
and theory, the culminating learning experience is often a practicum
out there in the so-called real
world. This is a type of curing
period for the student designed to
bring all of the academic knowledge

---

*Reprinted with permis-
sion of the author, Eliz-
abeth A. Daly. (Paper
presented at the annual
conference of the Inter-
national Congress for In-
dividualized Instruction,
Lafayette, Indiana, Nov.
6-8, 1977) (ED 151514)

into operation and testing in a
real environment. Indeed all
that preceded the practicum may
have been preparation for this
activity. Supervised teaching
for pre-service teachers and in-
hospital experiences for nurses
in training are common, traditional examples of such experiences.

Today it is common practice to
provide internship experiences in
such fields as business, banking,
social work, psychology, retail-
ing and public administration and
education. We will probably see
an increase of such programs in
the future as the internship real-
izes its potential as a learning
experience in many diverse fields.

Too often students involved in
an internship wander aimlessly or
are herded impersonally through
real world experiences unsuper-
vised by a faculty member and un-
related to the academic world by
any guidance system. Internship
students must be guided by someone familiar with the academic
training received by the student
and with experience in the real
situation into which the student
will be submerged in toto for
an extended period of time. The
task of preparing the student for
the total real world environment
falls on the faculty supervisor.
A vital part of any internship
takes place on campus in the
briefing of the student before
he enters the new situation.
Once the student enters the real
environment, the supervisor must
continue to guide and support the
student if the maximum benefit is
to be derived from this learning
activity. Without preparation
and continuing liaison, the internship degenerates into an in-
teresting, time-consuming happening having little long-range
impact on the student.

A log properly kept by the student and carefully considered by
the faculty supervisor serves to
individualize and intensify the
effect of the internship as the
student seeks to integrate theory
and reality. The potential

exists for a log to be the vehicle to provide the student with a completely individualized experience, a support and guidance system, and a personalized relationship with a faculty member.

Precise objectives for the actual participation observation and recording of the experiences should be developed with the student prior to the beginning of the practicum. Usually the student is insensitive to the raison d'etre for the internship. He enters the real world because that is what his program of courses stipulates. The reasons for keeping a log need to be clearly delineated or it becomes merely a chore to be completed to satisfy an academic requirement. In general, a log is maintained to record in a clinical manner exactly what happens in real life and to analyze in a knowledgeable, but unique way the meaning of what one has experienced.

Maintaining the clinical observations is often easy for students of the natural, quantitative, and behavioral sciences for they are trained in this skill. Students of the liberal arts and social sciences sometimes experience difficulty separating what they experience from what they feel. On the other hand, students in the sciences may fail to react with depth to their observations while the student of English or history may tend to be stirred emotionally more than rationally. Both of these situations indicate the need for guidance to the student.

Differentiated and articulated goals meeting individual needs are vital for the same practical experience may serve vastly different goals for different students. Three trainees, one each in geriatric nursing, clinical psychology and social welfare might spend time participating and observing in a home for the aged. Each would probably have vastly different sub-objectives although the overall objective of serving the needs of the elderly might be a common goal.

Through individual logs, the unique goals of different students may be met even though they may be having similar or even the same basic experiences. Instructions may be individualized by differentiating focal points for the observers. Reactions to such experiences are idiosyncratic by nature, and therefore instruction is further individualized.

When the experience of each student is unique, the journal enhances the individuality of the already existing custom-made learning experience. For example, when one student of social welfare goes to a home for the aged, one to a pediatric ward of a hospital, and one to a social club for the aged, each experience is unique and through the log the experience becomes even more made-to-order.

At the outset, a systematic, logical, and regular means by which experience and reactions should be recorded must be clear to the student. Observations which clinically state experience and behavior should be separated from the accompanying value-laden reactions of the student. The difference between, "What is," and "What ought to be," must be recognized before the student is ready to write meaningful log entries. It should be clear to the student that all people in the same situation would record basically the same behavior with perhaps differing emphases depending upon the objectives of the practicum. Conversely, it must be equally clear that all people in the same situation would react in a special manner based on personal values, beliefs, past experiences, biases, and perceptions. The value of the student's singular reaction must be stressed for in the real world the practitioner will behave independently of the teacher. It is important for that process to begin in the log, as this is in preparation for behavior in the real world where the risk-taking is much greater and the support and guidance system almost non-existent. The supervisor must have a genuine respect for the reactions of the student, but must also seek the bases for these reactions.

An effective format is to write the clinical observation on the left page with the accompanying personal reaction directly opposite on the right page. Using this format the writer and reader may easily correlate observation and accompanying reaction without confusion. A serious error occurs when logs are written in a manner which merges observations and reactions. One or the other tends to dominate and reality and fantasy mesh in an indecipherable manner resulting in grand confusion.

A time-table for recording and sharing the log entries should be established in the beginning. Under no circumstances should a log remain unread by the supervisor until the end of the internship.

Prompt recording after each session prevents the observation from becoming stale or superficial due to the forgetting curve. Reactions written simultaneously to the recording of the observations tend to preserve the emotional, critical, cathartic nature of the human response which occurred internally at the time of the observation. This candid, visceral response of the student is one of the most important effects of the internship. Cleansed, censored reactions designed to match those of the supervisor are devoid of real worth to either participant in the log-keeping process, student or instructor.

Regular, prompt, written and oral feedback to the students from the instructor is advisable in order to maximize benefits from the log-keeping. Instructors should provide either type of feedback to the student within a week's time or the impact is diminished. Written comments should be used supplemented by conferences when possible.

Judgmental reactions by the instructor should be kept to a minimum, particularly at first, to assure that the student's reactions are not stifled or programmed to meet the judgments of the more experienced member of the internship team. The practicum is designed to lessen dependency, not increase it. Therefore circumspection is required when offering feedback. Questions rather than statements tend to stimulate the emotional growth of the student's perception of reality, critical thinking, and analysis of situations and self.

As the student comes to realize the value of his own independent analysis of his experience, the instructor may reveal his own value judgments concerning the situation. It is helpful if the instructor labels his reactions as value judgments. This reminds the student that value judgments are NOT correct or incorrect; they are correct for whomever makes them.

To maximize the effect of the supervisor's comments, the log entries submitted weekly or bi-weekly should be carefully read, annotated and returned to the student. Any written questions of the instructor in the log should be answered in writing by the student as soon as possible. Desirably the two will have an opportunity to discuss directly their reactions, comments, and questions, but written feedback and student response to that feedback assures a written dialogue which is valuable in lieu of oral dialogue. With some students, written interaction is more candid and open than direct interaction for the environment is less threatening than being in the physical presence of the instructor forced to react within a brief time.

At all times, inaccurate factual data should be corrected by the instructor or the student should be directed to sources of information. Data and judgments are treated differently for they are greatly dissimilar.

Criteria for the formal evaluation of the log need to be established when objectives, procedures, and guidelines are defined. Dependent upon situational factors, basic criteria might include:
. regular entries in the log
. separation of observations and reactions
. in-depth analysis of observations
. objective perceptions of reality
. effective communication of ideas
. reactions based on knowledge and rationality as well as individual emotional responses
. justification of reactions
. formation of valid conclusions based on data
. separation of significant events from trivia
. focal points for internship were maintained
. objective self analysis.

The final entry in any log should be an overall, penetrating analysis of the totality of the real life experience in terms of past knowledge, theory, and attitudes as tested against the present world of the internship. It is quite probable that predictions for the future performance of practitioners in the given field might be made particularly for the future of the student within that realm. In essence, the student ought to seek an answer to the sociologist's basic question, "Now that I know what is out there, so what?"

Desirably this ending entry should be discussed at length with the instructor. After final formal evaluation of the log, it should be returned to the student in the anticipation that it may serve a worthwhile function in the future if the practitioner chooses to review and re-evaluate his initial experiences in the field.

Various effects result from the process of keeping a log: learning objectives in all three domains may be met. In addition to cognitive and psychomotor objectives, the often neglected affective domain is included in the student's reacting to his own observations. Students also learn to write creatively, to think for themselves, and test their beliefs and values.

There is no question that journals demand a great deal of effort by the student, the instructor, and the supervisor, but the amount, nature, and quality of the learning indicates an extremely high return to both participants for the investment.

Individualizing instruction means providing a unique learning experience appropriate to the needs, interests, and abilities of the student. Logs are an effective means of individualizing the learning resulting from an internship.

## THE RÉSUMÉ...YOUR PASSPORT TO AN INTERVIEW*
Frank R. Braun

The résumé is an essential first step in the process of securing a new position. Sometimes referred to as a vita or a personal data sheet, the résumé is defined in a standard dictionary as a "brief account of one's educational and professional experience," "a summing up," "an abridgement" or a "condensed statement." Preparing a résumé serves both to assist you in a review of your personal assets, strengths, and qualifications and to present these special attributes in the most favorable way to a prospective employer. To accomplish both purposes, you must first know a great deal about yourself and the position for which you plan to be a successful applicant. The well prepared résumé should convince the employer that you are a "perfect" match for the position. Accomplishing this in a résumé is difficult work; take the time to review

_____

*Included in the 1980 edition of ASCUS "Teaching Opportunities For You." ASCUS, Association for School, College and University Staffing, P.O. Box 4411, Madison, WI 53711.

thoroughly your qualifications before beginning the preparation. Presented here are some basic steps and suggested content to assist you.

### Why Prepare a Résumé?

Is your placement file not enough? Will you not be duplicating the information that is already in the placement file or on an employer's application? The answer is yes, but in a résumé you will present yourself in the most advantageous manner and in your own unique way.

### Some Uses of the Résumé

A well-prepared résumé serves several uses that can assist you in your search.

1. to serve as a general introduction to accompany your brief original letter of inquiry or application.
2. to introduce you in any chance meeting with a potential employer; such as, a conference, the PTA, a neighborhood political meeting or a family reunion! Use this résumé as a "calling card."
3. to add information detailing your background and experience in a follow-up of an earlier contact.
4. to facilitate an interview. Take extra copies of your résumé with you to an interview; offer them to members of an interview committee who might not have had the chance to read your placement file. In this manner, you may call attention to items you consider important--items that may be overlooked in the limited time reserved for an interview or become lost due to "memory lapse."
5. to become part of your placement file. You may want the résumé to become part of the documentation in your file

that is sent to employers to support your application.

### Stages in the Preparation of the Résumé

Writing the résumé involves three stages--

1. <u>Research</u>--know both yourself and the position sought.
2. <u>Organization</u>--arrange the various pieces of information about yourself into categories: such as, personal data, education, experience, recognitions, special skills, travel, writing, and publications.
3. <u>Production</u>--select paper stock, color, printing, and arrangement on the page to present a pleasing, easily read final copy that reflects your personal style.

### "Functional" or "Chronological" Résumé?

Résumés may be organized to emphasize a chronological record of experiences and events or they may be organized around functional skills and abilities. The "chronological" résumé is appropriate for the person of limited experience with an easily described record of training leading to a specific professional field. The "functional" résumé is useful for the person with broad experiences who wishes to emphasize specialized skills and to identify details that have applicability to a variety of positions. Skills such as writing, managing, consulting or research are considered important in the job market.

Both the "functional" and the "chronological" résumé require the writer to proceed through the three stages--research, organization and production, and to follow the rules of résumé writing given below:

1. <u>Economy</u>--Keep the résumé brief! One page is the ideal. People with wide experience and many qualifications may require more than one page.

2. <u>Supportiveness</u>--Be positive in your word choice. State firmly and frankly your qualifications. Use action words. Convey enthusiasm.
3. <u>Completeness/Selectivity</u>-- This may appear to be a contradiction: it isn't. Don't overlook important details in your qualifications. But be selective.
4. <u>Accuracy</u>--Keep in mind that anything you put in a résumé may be checked by an employer or be the subject of questioning in an interview.
5. <u>Acceptability</u>--Select paper stock and color to give the best first impression. Choose type face and printing method that will read easily. Organize content so that the reader can quickly scan the résumé to find the essential elements.
6. Chronology--The reverse chronological order listing the current or most recent position first and then moving backward in time is the preferred pattern. Employers generally place the greatest emphasis on current or most recent employment.
7. <u>Creativity</u>--Your finished résumé should distinguish you from the other applicants. To do this and still follow generally accepted rules of résumé writing is a challenge. Here is your chance to give the essential qualifications and still present something of yourself.

### Content

The purpose and uses of the résumé determine the content. Focus the content on the position you are seeking. Emphasize those elements in your experience and preparation that qualify you for the position you seek. Here are some items considered to be of value in the résumé.

Personal identification--Basic information includes name, address and telephone number. Beyond this essential data, the decision on what additional information of a personal nature you wish to provide is your choice.

Professional preparation--Colleges attended, dates of attendance, diploma and degree earned (with dates); certificates or licenses held or eligible for by date of employment, such as, teaching licenses, special endorsements, coaching certificates, the W.S.I., etc.; student teaching, internships or teaching experience. Give brief details on location, name of school, grade or subject and dates of these professional experiences.

Special skills--Briefly mention those areas in which you can provide leadership; such as, athletics, recreation programs, art, crafts, speech, dramatics.

Interests--Hobbies and recreational activities.

Memberships--Honors, scholarships and awards--high school, college, community and public service.

Miscellaneous--Summer employment, military or volunteer experiences, work, travel and projects which you initiated. Choose from among these experiences one or several to mention briefly to encourage the reader to know more about you.

Finally, identify clearly the name and mailing address of your college placement office from which the employer may request your placement file.

Style, Appearance, Format

You have now selected the content of your résumé; next carefully phrase the information into brief statements in the telegraphic or outline writing style. Use a minimum of words to tell your story. Readability is enhanced by leaving ample open space on the page to emphasize the content. Résumés should never be xeroxed but rather photo offset. Check the Yellow Pages of your local telephone book for professional typists and offset printing services. The typing of the copy may be done with several typefaces to add variety and emphasis to your résumé.

Many colors and several different varieties of paper stock are generally available. Although white paper is by far the most frequently used, your résumé may attract more favorable attention on tan or beige paper. Use a good quality paper, perhaps with a pebble or textured surface.

Finally--review and revise; no résumé improves merely with age. Share your résumé with others; check it out with the "pros." Go beyond the college placement office to also ask school employing officials, student teaching supervisors, and administrators for opinions and advice.

The résumé is an essential tool in your introduction to career opportunities. Make it serve to your best advantage. It will not secure the job for you, but will help you obtain the interview and consideration for the position.

Your résumé also serves as the basis for a constant review of your career plans and for your continued success in the future.

Part Four

## EVALUATION AND RESEARCH IN FIELD-BASED LEARNING

> There are many truths of which the full mean-
> ing cannot be realized until personal experi-
> ence has brought it home.
>
> - John Stuart Mill

## Introduction

The earlier sections of this book have provided an overview of the world of work in postsecondary learning organizations, they have presented a review of learning models and research which have application to field-based education, and they have outlined a program for implementing a postsecondary internship. Part Four deals with the process of learning from experience through evaluation and research.

Chapter 8 describes an evaluation model which includes the assessment of various outcomes of the internship experience. Those persons who plan and conduct field-based learning experiences may not wish to use the suggested procedures and forms in their entirety. However, the evaluation model should be useful in the development of alternative procedures or instruments. The two selected readings in Part Four, by Whitaker and Angus, discuss additional considerations regarding the evaluation of field-based learning programs.

Chapter 9 presents the results of a research study with participants in a postsecondary practicum similar in design to the internship model described in this book. The study is exploratory in nature, and it raises a number of questions regarding key issues in experiential learning. Readers are encouraged to extend the thrust of this research into related areas so that the empirical and theoretical foundations of field-based learning design might be progressively strengthened.

Chapter 8

## FOCUS ON EVALUATION

> Experience enables you to recognize a mistake
> when you make it again.
>
> - Franklin P. Jones

In order to learn from experience, evaluation is a necessity. Following Angus (1974; see Selected Reading, p. 134), the evaluation component
of the field experience described in this volume has two objectives:
"To evaluate the student's performance as to skill development, knowledge and experience acquisition and work accomplished, and to evaluate
the effectiveness of the various elements of the total program in accomplishing its goals."

The evaluation plan presented in this chapter distinguishes between
formative evaluation and summative evaluation. As Scriven (1967) has
pointed out, the formative role of evaluation is one of on-going improvement, while the summative role contributes directly to the making
of final judgments and decisions. Formative evaluation helps to improve
learning in progress; summative evaluation assesses what the quality of
that learning has been. Of course, summative evaluation can be formative in the larger context of lifelong learning, but it is final with
respect to the present learning episode.

Figure 4 presents the Evaluation Model for this Internship in Postsecondary Education. Five targets of evaluation are identified: (1)
Participants' Cognitive Learning, (2) Participants' Affective Learning;
(3) Participants' Applicative Learning; (4) Program Quality; and (5)
Instructor and Field Supervisor Roles. For each target, performance
indicators, key evaluators, formative approaches, and summative approaches to evaluation are identified.

### Participants' Cognitive Learning

While a major thrust of experiential learning is to develop skills and
attitudes, cognitive learning is also an important goal of the internship experience. With the aid of the "Preliminary Learning Goals Formulator" (Appendix B) each participant sets objectives for the attainment
of knowledge and the application of prior cognitive learning to practical situations. Performance indicators for cognitive learning include
the following:

Figure 4: INTERNSHIP IN POSTSECONDARY EDUCATION EVALUATION MODEL

| Evaluation Targets | Performance Indicators | Key Evaluators | Formative Approaches | Summative Approaches |
|---|---|---|---|---|
| Participants' Cognitive Learning | -Set and achieve cognitive learning goals<br>-Apply concepts to work experience<br>-Organize and present ideas effectively | -Instructor<br>-Supervisor(s)<br>-Participants<br>-Peers | -Instructor/participant conferences<br>-Log entries<br>-Project proposal<br>-Participant/supervisor conferences<br>-Seminars | -Self-evaluation of goals<br>-Exploration papers/articles<br>-Log entries<br>-Final project report<br>-Participant Assessment by Instructor<br>-Oral report of experiences<br>-Visitation report |
| Participants' Affective Learning | -Work with people<br>-Handle stress<br>-See and respect others' points-of-view | -Supervisor(s)<br>-Participants<br>-Instructor<br>-Peers | -Supervisor observation<br>-Instructor observation<br>-Participant/supervisor conferences<br>-Participant/instructor conferences<br>-Sharing with peers | -Self-evaluation of goals<br>-Field supervisor feedback form<br>-Participant Assessment by Instructor |
| Participants' Applicative Learning | -Formulate and attain work goals<br>-Develop task skills<br>-Manage time<br>-Formulate career goals | -Supervisor(s)<br>-Instructor<br>-Participants<br>-Peers | -Supervisor observation<br>-Instructor observation<br>-Participant/supervisor conferences<br>-Participant/instructor conferences<br>-Sharing with peers | -Logs with attachments<br>-Final project report<br>-Self-evaluation of goals<br>-Field supervisor Feedback Form<br>-Participant Assessment by Instructor |
| Program Quality | -General internship goals<br>-Value to participants<br>-Value to host organizations<br>-Participant placement | -Participants<br>-Supervisor(s) | -Participant/instructor conferences<br>-Supervisor/instructor conferences | -Program evaluation form<br>-Internship perception questionnaire<br>-Follow-up survey |
| Instructor/Field Supervisor Roles | -Provide resources<br>-Provide help<br>-Enhance learning climate<br>-Evaluate effectively | -Participants<br>-Supervisor(s)<br>-Instructor | -Participant/instructor conferences<br>-Participant/supervisor conferences<br>-Supervisor/instructor conferences<br>-Instructor/supervisor interim feedback form | -Program evaluation form<br>-Internship perception questionnaire |

- Ability to set and achieve cognitive learning goals.
- Ability to apply concepts to work experience.
- Ability to organize and present ideas effectively.

Key evaluators of participant cognitive learning include the instructor, field supervisor(s), the participant, and the participant's peers.

Formative evaluation approaches in this area take several forms. Throughout the internship, the instructor and participant hold individual conferences to discuss progress toward cognitive learning goals and how theoretical concepts might relate to work experiences. When the log entries or Project Proposal are submitted to the instructor, these are reviewed and discussed with the participant and new cognitive learning goals are set as appropriate. See the "Internship Log Feedback Form" (Appendix H). Periodic conferences between the participant and field supervisor may be used for similar formative evaluation purposes. Finally, seminars on topics related to postsecondary education and leadership may be held from time to time throughout the internship. The seminars provide opportunity for participants to interact with each other, with guest speakers, and with the instructor regarding pertinent research, concepts, and theoretical constructs.

There are a number of ways in which participants' cognitive learning can be evaluated summatively. The "Learning Goals Self-Evaluation Form" (Appendix C) is completed by each participant near the end of the internship. In addition, Exploration Papers, articles for publication, log entries, the Final Project Report, the report of the observational visit, and the oral report are all indications of participants' achievement of cognitive learning goals. Refer to "Assessment of Final Log Entries" (Appendix G) and "Assessment of Final Project Report" (Appendix I). In addition, the "Participant Assessment by Instructor" (Appendix L) contains a section on assessment of participants' cognitive learning.

## Participants' Affective Learning

Key performance indicators in this area are:

- Ability to work with people.
- Ability to handle stress.
- Ability to see and respect others' points of view.

The field supervisor(s), participants themselves, their peers, and the instructor are in positions where they can assist in the evaluation of this learning area. Formative approaches include observation of the participant by the field supervisor(s) and instructor, coupled with periodic discussions at conferences between them. In addition, meetings should be scheduled from time to time to enable internship participants to share feelings about their experiences and attitudes toward work and co-workers. The "Instructor/Field Supervisor Interim Feedback Form" (Appendix K) may be useful in structuring such meetings.

Summative approaches to the area of participants' affective learning include the pertinent section of the "Learning Goals Self-Evaluation Form" (Appendix C), the "Field Supervisor Feedback Form" (Appendix M), and the "Participant Assessment by Instructor" (Appendix L).

## Participants' Applicative Learning

One of the major goals of an internship or any field-based learning experience is that the participants be able to function as professionals in whatever field they are working. Hence, key performance indicators in this area are:

- Ability to formulate and attain work goals.
- Development of task area skills.
- Ability to manage time effectively.
- Ability to formulate career goals.

Once again, field supervisors, the instructor, the participants themselves, and peer learners can be helpful in evaluating learning in this area. Periodic formal and informal meetings between participants, field supervisors, and instructor can be especially helpful in providing formative evaluation in this area. Sharing-sessions among peers can also provide insight into additional ways of solving problems or dealing with issues on the job.

There are a number of approaches to summative evaluation of applicative learning. The log entries with appropriate attachments or the Final Project Report should indicate the degree to which work goals were achieved. The "Assessment of Final Log Entries" (Appendix G) or "Assessment of Final Project Report" (Appendix I) should be completed by the instructor. In addition, the "Learning Goals Self-Evaluation Form" (Appendix C), the "Field Supervisor Feedback Form" (Appendix M) and the "Participant Assessment by Instructor" (Appendix L) contain sections dealing with applicative learning.

## Program Quality

An important aspect of the internship to be evaluated is the overall quality of the program itself. Not only can the program be improved over time as the result of successive summative evaluations, but the internship for any group of participants can be improved in process through timely feedback. Key performance indicators of program quality include the following:

- General goals of the internship.
- Value to participants.
- Value to host organizations.
- Placement of participants.

The participants and the field supervisors are the primary sources of information in this evaluation component. Through periodic meetings and telephone conversations between the instructor and field supervisor(s), and between participants and instructor, indications of program quality can be gained in time to make appropriate changes if needed.

The "Program Evaluation Form" (Appendix N) has been designed to obtain summative evaluation data regarding program quality. The Internship Perception Questionnaire (IPQ) (Appendix P) is a research-oriented instrument that will provide group data regarding program quality. The "Follow-up Survey" (Appendix O) is designed to be sent to participants six months to a year following their completion of the internship experience in order to collect information about the placement of participants.

## Instructor and Field Supervisor Roles

Crucial to participant learning are the roles of the instructor and field supervisor(s). Key performance indicators for effectiveness in these roles are the following:

- Ability to provide resources to participants.
- Ability to provide help as needed.
- Ability to enhance the learning climate.
- Ability to evaluate effectively.

Through periodic meetings with the participants, the instructor and field supervisor(s) should solicit feedback about participants' perceptions of their role effectiveness. While this may be difficult to do because of real and perceived status and power differentials, the use of the "Instructor/Field Supervisor Interim Feedback Form" (Appendix K) may be helpful in eliciting formative feedback in this area.

Summative evaluation information about the roles of instructor and field supervisor(s) may be obtained by use of the "Program Evaluation Form" (Appendix N) and the Internship Perception Questionnaire (Appendix P).

## Evaluation in Perspective

While grades are necessary in some internship experiences because of institutional policy or credential needs, the grade should be determined as a result of an evaluation process that enhances the total learning experience. While the various components of the evaluation model presented in this chapter may not be used in exactly the same manner by all those conducting field-based learning experiences, the intent of the model is to assure that helping, rather than judging, is the key evaluative process, and that learning, rather than grading, is the key evaluative outcome.

Chapter 9

A RESEARCH STUDY OF EXPERIENTIAL LEARNING

> The one real objective of education is to
> have a man in the condition of continually
> asking questions.
>
> - Bishop Mandell Creighton

In Chapter 3 of this volume, the ideas of Barbara Hursh and Lenore
Borzak, Allen Tough, and David Kolb were presented as the bases for new
approaches to experiential learning. The present chapter reports a research study dealing with the application of some of those researchers'
concepts to an internship experience. It would be helpful to refer to
Chapter 3 for definitions of terminology and conceptual clarification
during the reading of this study.

Almost any collegiate or professional program can be viewed in light
of experiential learning theory. Since 1971, the College of Education
at The Cleveland State University (CSU) has offered a master's degree
program in postsecondary educational instruction, administration, and
counseling. As in many other similar programs, the CSU program included a substantial field experience (Practicum) component. Until recently, the Practicum was relatively undefined and unstructured. Participants were placed in an institution or organization in an employment
field matching their career objectives, but the content and quality of
their learning experiences were not carefully planned or closely moni-
tored.

During the 1977-78 academic year, the Practicum in the CSU Postsecondary Program was redesigned based on some of the ideas in the
emerging learning models discussed earlier in Chapters 2 and 3. Participants in the revised Practicum were called upon to carefully assess
their competence as postsecondary educators based upon prior professional experiences and the knowledge and skills gained through graduate
course work. This information was compared with competencies required
in the participants' anticipated career roles. Where deficiencies in
either knowledge or skill existed, the participants, with the help of
the university instructor and on-site supervisors, planned experiential
learning activities to be undertaken.

Each Practicum participant formulated a learning contract consisting
of a number of experiences at four levels of involvement. At least
five experiences were included at the observation level and five at the

interview or discussion level. In addition, each person planned six or
more projects at a limited participation level, where he or she would
gain hands-on experience over a number of days or weeks. Two major
projects, where the participant assumed primary responsibility for
results, became a part of each learning contract. Through the learning contracts, participants were encouraged to experience the complexity of the professional environment and to gain a variety of insights
regarding their own capabilities and desires.

The participants' on-site learning experiences were analyzed and evaluated for the purposes of assessing student success as practitioners,
the ability to relate theory and practice, and the achievement of stated
learning goals. Several methods of analysis and evaluation were used,
including demonstrations of competence, reviews of accomplishments within
the organization, written interpretive analyses, and instructor and
supervisory comments. Ultimately, information gained through analysis
and evaluation was used to establish employment credentials and to build
job search skills.

## Design for the Study

In order to compare participants' perceptions of the character and
quality of their learning experiences under the original and revised
Practicum models, a questionnaire study was undertaken by Brent
Poppenhagen, Ernest Schuttenberg, and John Gallager, all from the CSU
College of Education. A survey instrument, the Internship Perception
Questionnaire (IPQ), was developed by the researchers based on concepts
of Hursh and Borzak, and Tough (see Chapter 3). Forty-six items were
employed in the construction of eight subscales corresponding to the
constructs of (a) decentering, (b) reciprocity, (c) holistic thinking,
(d) sense of self-competence (Hursh and Borzak), (e) self-directed
learning approach, (f) self-directed learning skills, (g) rewards of
learning, and (h) obtaining relevant help for learning (Tough). Total
scores on these subscales served as dependent variables. The IPQ instrument and the items selected for each subscale are reproduced as
Appendixes P and Q.

The IPQ, together with Kolb's (1976) Learning Style Inventory (LSI),
was sent to sixty-three persons who had completed the Practicum. Forty-
two participants had completed the earlier version of the Practicum
while 21 had experienced the revised version. Together, the two groups
comprised the total population of Practicum enrollees for 1978 and
1979. The return rate of the instrument was 23 (55%) for the earlier
Practicum and 20 (95%) for the revised Practicum. Participants ranged
in age from 22 to 58. The average age was 34. Eighty-seven percent
(20) of the earlier Practicum and 75 percent (15) of the revised Practicum groups were female, reflecting the program's overall female
enrollment majority.

## Hypotheses

A series of hypotheses related to predictions generated by the theoretical positions of Hursh and Borzak, Tough, and Kolb, were tested in
the study. Consistent with Hursh and Borzak, it was hypothesized that
when compared with persons completing the earlier Practicum, persons
completing the revised Practicum would show higher mean scores on subscales of the IPQ designed to measure the characteristics of (a) decentering, (b) reciprocity, (c) holistic thinking and (d) sense of self-
competence.

122

As would be predicted by Tough's theoretical perspective, it was conjectured that persons completing the revised Practicum would produce higher mean scores on IPQ subscales intended to measure (a) the use of self-directed learning approach, (b) self-directed learning skills, (c) rewards of learning, and (d) obtaining relevant help for learning than would their counterparts experiencing the earlier Practicum.

The usefulness of Kolb's taxonomy of learning styles was evaluated in a series of hypotheses exploring the relationship of Kolb's learning styles and scores on the IPQ subscales of (a) decentering, (b) reciprocity, (c) holistic thinking, (d) sense of self-competence, (e) self-directed learning approach, (f) use of self-directed learning skills, (g) rewards of learning, and (h) obtaining relevant help. These hypotheses were evaluated for the combined participants from both Practicum formats.

Findings

The four hypotheses generated by the theoretical posture of Hursh and Borzak were evaluated by a series of t-tests comparing the mean scores of early Practicum and revised Practicum groups on the four appropriate IPQ subscales.[1] The results of these tests are reported in Table 1.

Table 1

RESULTS OF T-TESTS COMPARING EARLIER AND REVISED PRACTICUM
PARTICIPANTS ON IPQ SUBSCALES OF DECENTERING, RECIPROCITY,
HOLISTIC THINKING, AND SENSE OF SELF-COMPETENCE

| Group | N | M | SD | df | t |
|---|---|---|---|---|---|
| | | Decentering | | | |
| 1* | 23 | 27.61 | 5.03 | 41 | 2.20+ |
| 2 | 20 | 30.90 | 4.75 | | |
| | | Reciprocity | | | |
| 1 | 22 | 25.27 | 4.73 | 39 | .44 |
| 2 | 19 | 25.84 | 3.30 | | |
| | | Holistic Thinking | | | |
| 1 | 23 | 12.48 | 3.31 | 41 | .43 |
| 2 | 20 | 12.85 | 2.18 | | |
| | | Sense of Self-Competence | | | |
| 1 | 23 | 10.78 | 3.03 | 41 | .42 |
| 2 | 20 | 11.15 | 2.62 | | |

* Group 1 is the earlier Practicum; Group 2 is the revised Practicum.

+ $p < .05$.

---

[1] The authors wish to acknowledge the contribution of Millicent Nuver in the collection, processing, and analysis of data reported in this study.

It should be noted that persons omitting responses to any question on a subscale were deleted from the analysis for that subscale. As a result, the N for each group varies somewhat from subscale to subscale.

One of the t-tests, that for decentering, was found to yield a significant result (t = 2.20, df = 41, p < .0338). It should be noted that in each of the four comparisons reported in Table 1, the direction of the differences between means favored the revised Practicum group. Also in each case, the standard deviations for the revised Practicum group scores were smaller than those for the earlier Practicum group, indicating a tendency for somewhat higher agreement among the scores of the revised Practicum group.

Table 2 reports the results of t-tests employed to evaluate the four hypotheses related to Tough's theoretical position. Two of these results proved to be significant, the use of self-directed learning approach (t = 2.22, df = 35, p < .033) and obtaining relevant help for learning (t = 2.67, df = 36, p < .011). Again it should be noted that the direction of the differences between means on the two remaining subscales favored the revised Practicum group. The standard deviations for the revised Practicum group again indicated a tendency for more consistent responses from this group when compared to the earlier Practicum participants.

Table 2

DIFFERENCES BETWEEN PARTICIPANTS IN EARLIER AND REVISED
PRACTICUMS ON USE OF THE SELF-DIRECTED LEARNING APPROACH,
SELF-DIRECTED LEARNING SKILLS, REWARDS FOR LEARNING, AND
OBTAINING RELEVANT HELP FOR LEARNING

| Group | N | M | SD | df | t |
|---|---|---|---|---|---|
| Use of the Self-Directed Learning Approach | | | | | |
| 1* | 17 | 22.71 | 3.27 | 35 | 2.22+ |
| 2 | 20 | 20.60 | 2.65 | | |
| Self-Directed Learning Skills | | | | | |
| 1 | 23 | 32.78 | 4.73 | 41 | .85 |
| 2 | 20 | 33.80 | 2.71 | | |
| The Rewards of Learning | | | | | |
| 1 | 23 | 22.65 | 4.63 | 41 | 1.25 |
| 2 | 20 | 24.10 | 2.49 | | |
| Obtaining Relevant Help for Learning | | | | | |
| 1 | 19 | 14.16 | 3.99 | 36 | 2.67++ |
| 2 | 19 | 17.00 | 2.36 | | |

* Group 1 is the earlier Practicum; Group 2 is the revised Practicum.

+ p < .05.

++ p < .01.

The usefulness of Kolb's taxonomy of four learning styles in predicting performance on the eight IPQ subscales was assessed by classifying each member of the combined Practicum groups as an accommodator, assimilator, converger, or diverger, on the basis of their scores on Kolb's Learning Style Inventory. Once the four groups were formed in this manner, a series of eight one-way Analyses of Variance was conducted comparing the mean scores of the four groups on each of the eight IPQ subscales described above. The results of these ANOVA's are reported in Table 3.

Table 3

ANALYSIS OF VARIANCE ON VARIOUS IPQ SCORES
BY THE FOUR LSI LEARNING STYLES

| IPQ Variables | Accommodators Mean (N) | Assimilators Mean (N) | Convergers Mean (N) | Divergers Mean (N) | F |
|---|---|---|---|---|---|
| Decentering | 30.5 (4) | 28.7 (14) | 31.0 (10) | 25.6 (10) | 2.19 |
| Reciprocity | 26.2 (4) | 26.3 (12) | 26.5 (10) | 23.2 (10) | 1.47 |
| Holistic Thinking | 14.5 (4) | 12.9 (14) | 13.2 (10) | 9.7 (10) | 6.69+ |
| Sense of Self-Competence | 12.0 (4) | 11.6 (14) | 11.3 (10) | 8.7 (10) | 2.92* |
| Self-Directed Learning Approach | 19.8 (4) | 21.7 (12) | 22.7 (10) | 19.9 (7) | 1.55 |
| Self-Directed Learning Skills | 32.5 (4) | 33.9 (14) | 35.1 (10) | 30.3 (10) | 4.43+ |
| Rewards of Learning | 24.0 (4) | 23.1 (14) | 24.6 (10) | 21.8 (10) | 1.08 |
| Obtaining Relevant Help for Learning | 16.0 (4) | 15.5 (12) | 16.5 (10) | 13.5 (8) | 1.16 |

* p < .05.

+ p < .01.

Three of the resulting F ratios proved significant, Holistic Thinking (F = 6.69, df = 3.34, p < .01), Sense of Self-Competence (F = 2.92, df = 3.34, p < .05), and Self-Directed Learning Skills (F = 4.43, df = 3.34, p < .01). From Table 3, it can also be noted that of the four groups defined by the LSI, the mean scores for the Divergers are lower than those for the other three groups on each of the eight IPQ subscales which formed the basis for comparison. Also of interest is the fact that Convergers produced the highest mean scores of the four groups in all but two (Holistic Thinking and Sense of Self-Competence) of the eight IPQ subscales.

## Discussion

The interpretation of the data reported above requires the consideration of several factors. As would be expected, the return rate of the IPQ instrument was notably higher for the revised Practicum group (95%) than for the earlier one (55%). This may have resulted in some non-representativeness of the earlier Practicum respondents, though the magnitude and influence of this condition cannot be estimated. Also, the relatively small sample sizes have the effect of reducing the power of the statistical tests employed. However, even with this lower power, a number of significant results were obtained.

Finally, the qualities of the IPQ itself must be considered. Items employed in the construction of the eight subscales were selected on the basis of face validity, drawing from the descriptions of the researchers themselves. In order to determine the psychometric validity of the subscales, it will be necessary to obtain data from a larger number of respondents in order to conduct a factor analysis of the item sets. In the absence of these data, it is possible to examine the patterns of intercorrelations among the subscales. These patterns provide some preliminary indication of the instrument's performance. These intercorrelations are reported in Table 4, which can be divided into three sections: intercorrelations among the four Hursh and Borzak subscales (S1 to S4), those among the four Tough subscales (S5 to S8), and the intercorrelations among both sets of subscales.

An examination of Table 4 indicates that the four Hursh and Borzak subscales are consistently intercorrelated. This finding is not surprising based on the theoretically close relationships among these constructs. For the subscales based on Tough's dimensions, there are also a number of intercorrelations. The Self-Directed Learning Approach subscale (S5), however, appears to be conceptually distinct from the Rewards of Learning (S7) and the Obtaining Relevant Help for Learning (S8) subscales.

It is difficult to interpret the intercorrelations among the subscales in both sets. One noteworthy finding is that the Self-Directed Learning Approach subscale (S5) does not correlate significantly with any of the Hursh and Borzak subscales. Further evaluation of the eight subscales must await a more formal analysis based on larger sample sizes.

The findings of the study suggest that efforts to redesign the Practicum experience to broaden participants' perspectives on the complexity of the world of practice and to appreciate the points of view of others (decentering) proved successful. Corresponding improvements in reciprocity were not shown, however. Without the synergistic effect of an improvement in both factors, Hursh and Borzak's theory would not lead to an expectation of heightened perceptions of either holistic thinking or sense of self-competence.

Table 4

INTERCORRELATIONS OF IPQ SUBSCALES

|     | S1* | S2 | S3 | S4 | S5 | S6 | S7 | S8 |
|-----|-----|----|----|----|----|----|----|----|
| S1  |     | .564+++ | .426++ | .436++ | -.182 | .205 | .380++ | .642+++ |
|     |     | (43)** | (43) | (43) | (37) | (43) | (43) | (38) |
| S2  |     |    | .332+ | .679+++ | -.269 | .321+ | .511+++ | .356+ |
|     |     |    | (41) | (41) | (35) | (41) | (41) | (36) |
| S3  |     |    |    | .399++ | .219 | .517+++ | .358+ | .440++ |
|     |     |    |    | (43) | (37) | (43) | (43) | (38) |
| S4  |     |    |    |    | -.002 | .365+ | .440++ | .308 |
|     |     |    |    |    | (37) | (43) | (43) | (38) |
| S5  |     |    |    |    |    | .460++ | .051 | -.209 |
|     |     |    |    |    |    | (37) | (37) | (36) |
| S6  |     |    |    |    |    |    | .664+++ | .388++ |
|     |     |    |    |    |    |    | (43) | (38) |
| S7  |     |    |    |    |    |    |    | .552+++ |
|     |     |    |    |    |    |    |    | (38) |
| S8  |     |    |    |    |    |    |    |    |

  \* S1 = Decentering, S2 = Reciprocity, S3 = Holistic Thinking, S4 = Sense of Self-Competence, S5 = Self-Directed Learning Approach, S6 = Self-Directed Learning Skills, S7 = Rewards of Learning, and S8 = Obtaining Relevant Help for Learning.

 \*\* (N).

  \+ $p < .05$.

 \++ $p < .01$.

+++ $p < .001$.

The revised Practicum was designed in such a way as to enable participants to plan learning projects, with the help of appropriate resource persons, based on a personal needs assessment. It was expected, therefore, that participants in the revised Practicum would show significantly higher scores on the subscales related to the four Tough hypotheses than would the earlier group.

Counter to expectations, however, the earlier Practicum group showed significantly higher scores on "Use of the Self-Directed Learning Approach" than did participants in the revised Practicum. Perhaps the more structured design of the revised Practicum, in providing guidelines not available to the earlier participants, actually inhibited to some degree the exercise of self-directed learning. On the other three subscales related to the Tough hypotheses (Self-Directed Learning Skills, The Rewards of Learning, and Obtaining Relevant Help for Learning), however, the mean scores favored the revised Practicum participants, and in the latter, significantly so. It may have been that the revised Practicum, while not casting participants as much on their own resources, enabled them to use the help of others more effectively. This rationale may explain why the rewards of learning (including pride of accomplishment, learning about one's own learning style, and usefulness for career preparation) were significantly higher for participants in the revised Practicum.

Based on Kolb's learning style theory, one would expect "Convergers" to thrive in a Practicum situation. The Convergers' strengths are Abstract Conceptualization and Active Experimentation, and they stress the practical application of ideas. However, because Convergers focus in on single "correct" answers and since they have somewhat narrow technical interests, one would expect a somewhat low score on decentering and reciprocity scales.

The reverse of these latter expectations was true in the present study. Of the four style groups, the Convergers showed the highest scores in Decentering and Reciprocity and also in the other subscales with the exception of Holistic Thinking and Sense of Self-Competence. The Convergers showed significantly higher Self-Directed Learning Skills than did those with the three other learning styles. These skills include developing and implementing one's own learning approach, seeking out appropriate learning resources, setting deadlines, managing time, and controlling the learning design. Use of these skills would appear to be congruent with the Converger's learning approach.

The Diverger, on the other hand, is strong in imaginative ability and is able to view situations from many perspectives. These qualities, together with the Diverger's interest in working with people, would suggest that persons with this learning style would be high on decentering, reciprocity, and holistic thinking.

Again, the results of the present study do not support these expectations. In the three areas mentioned above, persons with the Diverger learning style showed the lowest scores in all three areas and in holistic thinking, a significantly lower mean score than participants with the other learning styles.

Generally speaking, participants with the Diverger learning style showed the lowest mean scores in all eight subscales of the IPQ. Further study should be conducted to explore the relationships between the Diverger learning style and the various learning processes and outcomes measured by the IPQ.

Of the four learning styles identified by Kolb, the Accommodator, with strengths in Concrete Experience and Active Experimentation, should be most compatible with a Practicum experience. In the present study, there were only four persons with this "action orientation" to learning (perhaps a reflection of the kinds of students who select a master's program in postsecondary education). Accommodators were relatively high in decentering, holistic thinking, and sense of self-competence. Kolb's (1976) description of the Accommodator as "relying heavily on other people for information rather than on one's own analytic ability" (p. 7) is borne out by the high score on the "Obtaining Relevant Help for Learning" subscale.

## Areas for Further Study

This pilot study, though conducted using a limited population and a newly designed instrument, represents a first attempt at understanding the relationships among three experiential learning theories.

It would be of interest to replicate this study with larger numbers of participants. If one were to divide respondents into two groupings - one group having high scores on the decentering and reciprocity subscales and the other group having low scores on both factors - it would be possible to test the combined effect of the two processes on holistic thinking and sense of self-competence.

Further investigation should also be carried out as to the relationship between Tough's principles of self-directed learning projects and the design of postsecondary educational experiences in institutional settings. Some questions worth pursuing are the following: What kinds of structure are most helpful in promoting self-directed learning? How can the motivational factors characteristic of self-directed learners be applied most effectively in degree or certification programs? What kinds of "planners" are most helpful to students in promoting the skills of self-directed learning?

The relationships between the four Kolb learning styles and the Hursh and Borzak and Tough constructs have not been completely clarified by the present study. Once again, replication of this study with larger numbers of respondents would be a useful next step in providing additional insights.

## Conclusion

The research by Hursh and Borzak, Tough, and Kolb all suggests one conclusion: adults can play an important role in the teaching-learning transaction. For those who design learning programs for students in postsecondary education settings, the present study has revealed new dimensions of concern and a number of practical planning considerations.

Educators and students alike need to utilize the processes of decentering and reciprocity to see more clearly each others' learning needs and points of view and to collaborate effectively in the design of learning programs. Some of the insights revealed by study of self-directing learners should be applied more fully to the design of programs in the variety of postsecondary educational institutions. Finally, teachers and learners alike must become more aware of individual learning styles - not so much to segregate learners into separate instructional paths, but rather to begin to systematically meet the challenge of expanding the learning repertoires of maturing adult learners.

## RECOMMENDATIONS FOR IMPROVEMENTS IN SELECTING AND TRAINING ASSESSORS*
Urban G. Whitaker

First, requirements for post-secondary degrees should be stated in terms of competencies or other well-defined educational outcomes. To require students to complete a specific number of courses or a specific number of units is not sufficient to insure that they receive an appropriate education. Students individually and society generally are better served when the goal is, for example, exhibiting a specified level of literacy rather than passing a specified English course, or when the depth requirement is stated as a set of competencies, such as the ability to analyze a political problem, identify alternatives, and recommend a solution, rather than the passing of a specified number of units in political science.

The advantages of competency- or outcome-based learning programs

----

* Reprinted with permission of the publisher from Experiential Learning by Morris T. Keeton and Associates, San Francisco: Jossey-Bass, Inc., 1976 (originally appeared as portion of Chapter 12, pp. 220-223).

are not exclusively, or even primarily, related to assessment. To treat courses and other learning experiences as means rather than ends improves the learning process and facilitates assessment--provided that institutional procedures encourage explicit identification of learning goals, procedures, and evaluative techniques.

Second, all students should be required to develop affective and applicative competence in addition to cognitive competence. Field experience learning may be the best (and in some cases the only) way to develop affective and applicative competence. Adequate assessment techniques, depend on the particular configuration of each student's learning objectives. The assessment of experiential learning can be more effective if it is clear why, when, and how much experiential learning should be included in a student's educational plan.

Third, a statement of the learning objectives and methods of instruction, and a detailed proposal for evaluation, should be standard requirements for all courses. All parties to the learning process, including outside agency personnel in the case of field experience education, should be participants in the application of these conditions to the specific learning situation. Even in a well-administered program, learning objectives are too often stated in general terms and evaluation is too often treated as a purely summative process. A more serious problem, compounding the others, is that the learner is often excused from coresponsibility for determining objectives and excluded from participation in the process of assessing the outcome.

For experiential learning programs, all three elements--objectives, methods, assessment--present more difficult problems. At worst, it is experience itself (rather than learning) that is credited. And even in the best programs it is more difficult to specify and to implement instructional and evaluative methods in the field than it is on the campus. For experiential learning programs, it is particularly important for students and outside agency supervisors to participate in identifying objectives, planning the learning methods, and performing both formative and summative evaluation functions. Field personnel cannot be expected to serve as effective assessors of academically creditable learning unless they are aware of student educational objectives as well as agency purposes. Thus it is strongly recommended that learning experiences that involve an outside agency be supported by an agreement that specifies the agency role in achieving and assessing educational outcomes.

Fourth, the training of assessors and the development of effective assessment techniques should be given as high a priority as the training of teachers and the development of instructional methods. The best road to progress in the selection and training of more effective assessors is more conscious attention to the problem.

For its formative as well as its summative advantages, the training of assessors should be a continuing aspect of the educational program of all postsecondary institutions. Bloom, Hastings, and Madaus (1971) concur that "in spite of its complexity, evaluation appears to be one of the most important categories of education objectives in our society" (p. 205). What is needed is an assessment of assessment practices and then an effort to respond to weaknesses with appropriate training.

Faculty members of postsecondary institutions are key persons in the assessment process. Not only are they important as assessors, but their own performance is one of the important functions to be assessed, and they are in the best position to act as trainers of other potential assessors. Faculty development programs should include both training in self-

assessment and training in the assessment training of others, including learners, nonfaculty teachers, and subject matter experts.

The problem of training assessors should be attacked simultaneously on several fronts. A comprehensive faculty development program and the training of learners by their teachers have already been mentioned. How can these programs be encouraged, and what else ought to be done? At the minimum, both for prior learning and for sponsored field programs, the training of assessors ought to be considered a joint responsibility approached both individually and collectively by postsecondary education, foundations, governments at all levels, business, and community agencies. In addition, training in all aspects of the assessment process ought to become a standard part of graduate training programs that produce either future postsecondary faculty members or supervisory and management personnel. Moreover, training materials should be produced to faciliate either individual or group development in all aspects of assessment. The CAEL Working Papers, the Assembly workshops, and the faculty development project are major contributions toward the achievement of this goal.

Fifth, it should be standard institutional policy and practice to avoid assessment error by utilizing multiple assessors and multiple assessments. The ingredients of perfect assessment can seldom be found in a single assessor or blended properly in a single technique. Raines (1974), for example, concludes that "the faculty supervisor should take the initiative in evaluation. The assessment should seek wide participation by faculty members, student and agency staff. There is no one best method of evaluating field experience" (p. 44). Because teachers, learners, observers, and outside experts all have unique contributions to make to effective assessment, after careful review of the conditions of each case (a step-by-step model is recommended), a team of assessors should be chosen to insure that all essential strengths are adequately represented. And because it is rare to find all of the essential assessment strengths even in a carefully chosen team of assessors, and because it is difficult to find a single assessment technique that can cover every important aspect of the learning outcomes in a particular case, it is always desirable to have more than one assessment whenever possible. (For an analysis of the need for a core of assessment techniques, see Breen, Donlon, and Whitaker, 1975, p. 55). In addition, a distinction should be made between those participants in the assessment process who are qualified to conduct it--the primary assessors--and secondary assessors, whose role should be limited to providing information for the use of the primary assessors.

Finally, the assessment contributions of learners should be enhanced and utilized. Careful attention should be given to the determination of those assessment functions that learners themselves can and cannot perform effectively. Training provisions for learners should be built into educational programs for both formative and summative purposes. In sponsored programs, assessment should be a formal part of both the preparatory course of orientation program and the followup seminar.

For prior learning, a formal assessment course is strongly recommended. The faculty members and students should both be given credit for what they teach and learn about the process of evaluation. For example, a variable unit course entitled "Assessment of Experiential Learning" might be taken for one, two, three, or four units by students seeking credit for learning in military service, Peace Corps, Vista, intercultural travel and residence, work experience, or volunteer activities. The units would be awarded as credit in education for learning, during the course, about evaluation and assessment. At the conclusion of the course, additional units could be recorded as credit by evaluation (the course is the evaluation) in whatever fields and whatever amounts the instructor believes to be appropriate. Such an arrangement has the dual advantage of providing excellent training for both teacher and learner and of incorporating the payment for faculty assessment directly into the regular instructional program.

References

Baines, T.R. "The Faculty Supervisor." In J. Duley (Ed.), New Directions for Higher Education: Implementing Field Experience Education, No. 6. San Francisco: Jossey-Bass, 1974.

Bloom, B.S., Hastings, J.T., Madaus, G.F. Handbook of Formative and Summative Evaluation of Student Learning. New York: McGraw-Hill, 1971.

Breen, P., Donlon, T., and Whitaker, U. The Learning and Assessment of Interpersonal Skills: Guidelines for Administrators and Faculty. CAEL Working Paper No. 4. Princeton, N.J.: Educational Testing Service, 1975.

EVALUATING EXPERIENTIAL EDUCATION*
Edward L. Angus

> The evolutionary and non-traditional format of experiential education has resulted in a variety of techniques for assessing the learning of individual students.

If one asked the question, What does one want to learn, the next question would be how best to learn it. Four modes of learning come readily to mind: the traditional classroom/teacher; meditation; observation; and experience. Each may be appropriate for the learning task and the individual involved at a particular time. Also although the current organization of public education seems to ignore the fact, all people do not learn in the same way, nor do they consider what is offered to be learned as consistently appropriate with their individual needs. In contrast to classroom education, experientially based education generally demands that the learner establish his own learning agenda, where and how he will learn. That

*Reprinted with permission of the publisher from Implementing Field Experience Education, John Duley, Issue Editor, NEW DIRECTIONS FOR HIGHER EDUCATION No. 6, Jossey-Bass, Inc., 1974, pp. 77-84.

fact may be one of the significant factors involved in recent increased interest in experiential learning. It is also at the core of the innovative movement in education today, and a source of difficulty in evaluating field experience education.

This paper addresses the particular problem of how to evaluate experientially based learning, focusing on individual field learning experiences. I am not here concerned with evaluation for purposes of awarding academic credit for prior experiences. The context of this discussion is the service-learning model of field-based learning. In this situation the project or task on which the intern is working is meeting some public need. The student is receiving academic credit and probably some financial remuneration. Ideally, the intern is devoting full-time (forty hours a week for ten to fifteen weeks) to the internship, although other time arrangements might easily fall within this paper's scope.

Purpose. Evaluation generally has two objectives: to evaluate the student's performance as to skill development, knowledge and experience acquisition and work accomplished and to evaluate the effectiveness of the various elements of the total program in accomplishing its goals.

### Valuable Program Components Assuring Effective Evaluation

Clearly Defined Objectives. As with all education, clearly defined objectives are a necessity if any effective evaluation is to be accomplished. The participants in a particular experiential education project must agree to a set of specific learning objectives before the project begins. Without such goals, it is virtually impossible to evaluate the experience objectively. Ideally, these learning objectives should be generated by the student in collaboration with the appropriate faculty and agency personnel. The faculty member should see that the learning objectives are pedagogically sound and the agency's role is to ensure that the task element of the experience meets a public need.

Research by Kiel (1972) has substantiated that the clearer the learning objectives the greater the likelihood of a personally and intellectually fulfilling experience for the student. And if the task is meaningful to the student, his motivation is enhanced. Only the individual can learn; others may facilitate that learning but the desire to know originates within each person. Objectives serve to clarify the learning process. Needless to say, unanticipated events or consequences may occur during the field placement that alter the original objectives and such should not be overlooked in the evaluation process. Indeed, experiential education provides many more opportunities for accidental and incidental learning than do other modes, and this is seen as one of the strengths of that mode in moving students from being dependent to becoming independent learners.

Prefield Orientation. In order that students will know what is expected of them, what will be evaluated and how, and will be helped to maximize the learning potential available through the field experience a prefield orientation is valuable. One means is a workshop that stresses such themes as problem-solving techniques, failure expectation level, or decision-making skills. Another way is to assemble written, audio, and video materials in a learning resources center on subjects such as those just mentioned. A third approach is curricular. A course or parts of several courses that lead up to a field experience will serve to maximize its impact; for example, courses or modules might deal with research methods, interviewing techniques, operation of sophisticated audio or video equipment, organizational theory, a course in state and local government, folklore, or minority studies. The prefield orientation is held as soon as students can be brought together after their assignment. Length of the preparation depends on need. In my view, if a school or department is seriously committed to exposing a significant number of students to experiential education, part of the commitment ought to include mechanisms for prefield orientation. Evidence of the utility of such sessions may be found in specific professional programs, such as social work and teacher preparation, that include orientation and field experiences as part of the degree program.

The importance of prefield preparation to the evaluative process is that students can be expected to derive certain skills and knowledge as well as realistic expectations of the field experience. Final evaluations concerning field performance can then be made in light of the prefield training.

Individualized Learning Contract and Reading List. In the service-learning model of field experience education, as in others, the individualized learning contract is widely used. This permits and assures that the learning opportunities provided by a particular placement are identified and the learning objectives clearly specified. This clear specification of objectives makes evaluation possible and provides a means by which the relationship between theory and practice can be explored more fully. Such a contract is best developed by the student and his faculty advisor in consultation with the agency supervisor. Often included in the learning contract will be a reading list and some reporting mechanism for evaluation purposes. The importance and usefulness of readings lie in raising questions in the student rather than simply increasing general knowledge of some subject matter.

Evaluation of Student Performance. What follows is a report on some of the best practices I know about in evaluating student performance in field experience education. Used alone, no technique would provide sufficient evaluative information. These relevant methods are mostly nontraditional in the sense of the prevailing model of education.

1. Intermediate feedback. Periodic on-site visitations by the faculty advisor or field project

director can serve as ongoing evaluation, provide corrective and/or
motivational feedback, and assess
some aspects of intellectual growth.
Site visits can also provide information on the supervisor's attitudes
and the student's relationships with
other employees, as well as a check
on adherence to the initial goals.
If the learning objectives appear
altered, corrective measures can be
taken or revised objectives nego-
tiated. Such adjustments are essential so that the final evaluation
is related to the actual field experience. Periodic meetings, perhaps back on campus if convenient,
between the student and the faculty
advisor can also serve many of the
same purposes as well as other more
academic ones. For example, discussions of reading materials or
literature that relate to the experience as well as frank assessments by the student may be the
format of such meetings. These
meetings should not replace on-
site visits, however, for in addition to the value of seeing the
situation for oneself, such visits
by a faculty person reaffirm the
educational worth of the field experience to both the student and
the agency personnel. "He cared
enough to come and see me." If
visits are simply impossible, periodic written reports or even telephone conversations with the student and agency supervisor may accomplish similar results.

2. Seminars or workshops during
the field experience. "In-service"
workshops involving groups of interns are prevalent. While a variety of formats for such sessions
are used, general components would
include the following. One or more
faculty members, students, or possibly agency personnel would have
responsibility for the meetings.
Reading lists, duplicated materials,
lectures, and discussions that relate to the field placement or to
a body of knowledge relevant to the
experiences are used. For example,
one of the largest political internship programs, that of the CUNY system, includes seminars with readings
and discussions focused on specific

problems or ideas, such as executive decision making, strategies
for change, or the theory and
practice of community power. The
group meets for several hours one
or more times during the period
of the field experience. This
technique stresses relating a body
of knowledge to the experience
(emphasizing the experiential
learning dimension) and encourages
participants to reflect on and
contrast their personal (concrete)
experiences with the more conceptually abstract literature. A
variant would be to use these
sessions for skill development in
areas of felt need.

3. Critical incident writing.
This technique, described earlier
in this issue by Duley, is not
widely utilized but I find it
impressive. The Justin Morrill
program provides an excellent
description of this evaluative
device. Students are required
to submit (in writing) to the
program director nine critical
incident reports at the conclusion of their field study. These
describe specific situations and
actions taken that demonstrate
the utilization of what are termed cross-cultural skills. According to Morrill field study materials: "Since the critical inci-
dents are descriptions of individual students' behavior they can
also provide the students opportunities to examine their own
values (by values here is meant
virtues, principles, beliefs,
convictions, comforts, material
possessions, and desires /desires
for money, power, position, influence, status, education and
the respect of others/ which are
so important to the student that
they strongly influence or determine his decisions and behavior)
and how these affect their behavior. These reflections then become occasions for gaining self-
knowledge."

4. Maintaining a diary or
journal. The keeping of a daily
journal or diary is a technique
with both educational and evaluative worth. I have found that

136

most students need fairly strong urging to keep up their journals and not be discouraged because their initial entries are not "pearls of wisdom" or brilliant insights into theretofore unsolved problems. However, a well-kept journal, periodically reviewed and discussed by the intern and faculty counselor, can add significantly to the learning process. Like critical incident writing, reflections recorded in a journal also generate knowledge of self.

5. Exit interview or final written evaluation. The use of exit interviews or written evaluations by both the agency supervisor and the faculty counselor furnish useful immediate feedback for the student. A final interview can provide immediate rewards for the student and serve as a legitimation of a task accomplished. Discussions of the experience and constructive criticism by and of each of the three parties involved can stimulate the learning process while the experience is still fresh in all their minds. If a formal written evaluation is made of the student by either the supervisor or the faculty member, a discussion of that evaluation with the student may accomplish similar goals.

6. Was the job well done? This is a less formal procedure than the one indicated above but nonetheless a useful one. It is to ask the simple question, "Was the job well done?" Asked of the student, the faculty advisor, and the agency supervisor, along with why or why not, it will generate considerable evidence.

7. Written or final reports. Several types of final reports are in use. One is a written report in a form useful to the agency in which the student served. Such a report can serve as the focus of the student's work task. A second type is a final self-analysis (either written or oral) of the student's behavior and learning during and as a result of the field experience. Periodic or

progress reports are also common. They stimulate the intern to reflect periodically on progress toward stated goals. A fourth type of assessment is a group evaluation by peers of a student's report on the field experience.

8. Examinations. If cognitive mastery of an area is a principal concern and can be clearly identified as a result of the field experience, an examination or a series of tests is used to determine the student's competency.

9. Return or post-field experience seminars. Depending upon academic credit and course structures, post-field seminars may be a day or two of sessions at the conclusion of the field experience in which students reflect and report on their personal experiences or they may extend for a more lengthy period. Justin Morrill College, for example, uses the latter and their return seminar, the third of a three-semester sequence, focuses on values clarification. Merrill College (U.C., Santa Cruz) provides a variety of post-field options, including opportunities to speak to classes, work with students in pre-field orientations, or take specific courses relating closely to the field experience. Colleges using a post-field seminar clearly think that the learning dimensions of the field experience are maximized in this setting. There is little doubt that when a group of students who have had very diverse field experiences get together, there is vast potential for exploring various relationships, values clarification, and integrating the field experience with other courses, experiences, or bodies of knowledge.

10. Self-evaluation. Having the student do some serious reflection-what occurred, if and how values conflicts arose and were resolved, what was learned and how that related to other learning situations-can help him place the field experience in perspective. Discussions of such an evaluation between the faculty advisor and student can

serve to further highlight the learning that resulted.

Program Evaluation. The performance of students is not the only thing being evaluated in field experience education. Programs are being evaluated also. A number of survey instruments are in use to assess the learning opportunities provided and the consequences of the programs for students. A rather generalized form, developed by Dvid Kiel for the North Carolina Internship Office, evaluates learning opportunities provided by a service-learning internship. Other types of questionnaires are being developed to provide more specific data in such areas of concern as cost per credit hour, appropriate faculty load, contribution of the field placement to the total educational experience of the student, the impact of the program on the student's career or professional goal clarification. Instruments are also being developed to ascertain the extent of value clarification and cultural understanding which occurred as a result of the program. Longitudinal studies are being used to assess the long range impact of field experience education by following up students four to five years after graduation.

The student is not the only learner; supervisors and faculty also participate in the learning experience. If nothing is happening in the advisor's and the supervisor's head and heart, the learning situation is probably inadequate. How to determine this may be difficult, but a few questions asked of students, faculty, and agency supervisors about programs are: Did the supervisor and advisor raise "hard" questions for the intern; were they receptive to new ideas or ways of doing things; did they provide a workable task and a supportive environment for its accomplishment; and did they engage the student in searches for alternative paths to problem solving? Like students, not all supervisors or faculty advisors are natural inquirers and some, if not most, will need

assistance in further developing those skills. Workshops or other sessions can be a definite asset in this area. (The North Carolina Internship Office "Internship Style Description Form" has been found to be helpful in such workshops, particularly for goals clarification. Also, their publication "Skills for Effective Supervision of Interns" and "Skills for Effective Faculty Counseling of Service-Learning Interns" are useful tools.)

## Conclusion

As stated earlier, few if any of the above techniques by themselves will provide an adequate evaluation of field experience, and each program director or faculty member involved in evaluating and credentialing experiential education has certain local criteria to satisfy. Much remains to be accomplished in providing sufficient empirically based evidence for any single technique. It is my experience that the evolving nature of experiential education on many college campuses has caused continual shifts in emphasis. Because experiential education is nontraditional, innovative assessment techniques might serve best. At the same time, as Hedlund (1973, p. 8) has pointed out so succinctly, "greater effort must be made to communicate the findings and the results of theory-testing--theory building." For that to occur, more careful attention must be given to documenting the evaluative techniques employed. Although their concern is not unique in education today, those involved in field experience education are anxious to test and develop a theoretical base for experiential learning.

## References

Hedlund, R.D. "Internship Evaluation: A Review and Proposal." Public Service Internship News, May-June, 1973, 5-8.

Kiel, D.H. Student Learning Through Community Involvement. Atlanta: Southern Regional Education Board, 1972.

# REFERENCES

Angus, E.L.   Evaluating experiential education.   In Implementing Field Experience Education, 6th Sourcebook.   San Francisco:   Jossey-Bass, 1974.

Armstrong, J.S.   Teacher vs. learner responsibility in management education.   Unpublished paper, Wharton School, University of Pennsylvania, 1978.

Ausubel, D.P.   The psychology of meaningful verbal material.   New York: Holt, Rinehart, and Winston, 1968.

Bashook, P.G.   Perspectives on professions education.   Professions Education Researcher, 1979, 3, 2.

Blake, R.R.   Action research training lab.   Tenth Proceedings.   West Point, New York, 1960.

Borg, W.R.   Educational research:   an introduction.   New York:   Longman, 1963.

Borzak, L. & Hursh, B.   Integrating the liberal arts and professionalism through field experience:   a process approach.   Alternative Higher Education.   Fall, 1977, pp. 3-16.

Braun, F.R.   The resume...your passport to an interview.   ASCUS Teaching Opportunities for You, 1979, pp. 10-12.

Carnegie Commission on Higher Education.   Toward a learning society. New York:   McGraw-Hill, 1973.

Cheren, M.I.   Facilitating the transition from external direction to greater self-direction in learning in educational institutions: a case study in individualized open system postsecondary education. (Doctoral dissertation, University of Massachusetts, 1978).   Dissertation Abstracts International, 1973, 39/03A, p. 1362:   (University Microfilms No. DDK78-16246).

Corrigan, G.J.   Corporate training:   a career for teachers?   Phi Delta Kappan, 1980, 61, 328-331.

Cristiani, T.S., & Cristiani, M.F.   The application of counseling skills in the business and industrial setting.   Personnel and Guidance Journal, November, 1979, pp. 166-169.

Cross, K.P.  Accent on learning.  San Francisco:  Jossey-Bass, 1977.

Daly, E.A.  Using student journals to individualize instruction.
    (Paper presented at the annual conference of the International
    Congress for Individualized Instruction, LaFayette, Indiana,
    November 6-8, 1977), ED 151014.

Dubin, R., & Taveggia, T.  The teaching-learning paradox.  Eugene,
    Oregon:  Center for the Advanced Study of Educational Administra-
    tion, 1968.

Gagne, R.H.  The conditions of learning (2nd ed.).  New York:  Holt,
    Rinehart, and Winston, 1970.

Greenberg, E.  The community as a learning resource.  Journal of
    Experiential Education, 1978, 1, 22-25.

Gross, R.  The lifelong learner.  New York: Simon and Schuster, 1977.

Hampden-Turner, C.  Radical man:  The process of psycho-social devel-
    opment.  Garden City, New York:  Anchor Books, Doubleday and Co.,
    1971.

Hiemstra, R.  Lifelong learning.  Lincoln, Nebraska:  Professional
    Educators Publications, 1976.

Hodgkinson, H.L.  Issues for the eighties.  Proceedings of the Forum
    of the Association for Institutional Research, 1979, Air Executive
    Office, 314 Stone Building, Florida State University, Tallahassee,
    Florida.

Hoekstra, R.B.  Internships as a means of training educational leaders:
    an historical and contextual perspective.  Washington, D.C.:  Paper
    presented at the annual meeting of the American Educational Research
    Association, 1975.  (ERIC Document Reproduction Service No. ED 103999.)

Hursh, B. & Borzak, L.  Toward cognitive development through field
    studies.  Journal of Higher Education, January/February, 1979, 50,
    63-78.

Innovative graduate programs directory.  Saratoga Springs, New York:
    Empire State College, Learning Resources Center, 1976.

Jones, J.D.  Student personnel work:  current state and future direc-
    tions.  NASPA Journal, 1978, 15 (4), 2-11.

Kidd, J.R.  How adults learn.  New York:  Association Press, 1959.

Knowles, M.S.  The adult learner:  a neglected species.  Houston,
    Texas:  Gulf, 1973.

Kogan, N.  Educational implications of cognitive styles.  In G. S.
    Lesser (Ed.), Psychology and educational practice.  Glenview, Ill.:
    Scott Foresman, 1971.

Kolb, D.A.  Learning style inventory.  Boston:  McBer and Company,
    1976.

Kolb, D.A.  Student learning styles and disciplinary learning environments:  diverse pathways to growth.  In A. Chickering (Ed.), The future American college.  San Francisco:  Jossey-Bass, in press.

Kolb, D.A., & Fry, R.  Toward an applied theory of experiential learning.  In C. Cooper (Ed.), Theories of group processes.  New York:  Wiley, 1975.

Levine, A.  Handbook on undergraduate curriculum.  San Francisco:  Jossey-Bass, 1978.

Maslow, A.H.  Eupsychian management.  Homewood, Illinois:  Richard D. Irwin, Inc., and The Dorsey Press, 1965.

McGregor, D.  The human side of enterprise.  New York:  McGraw-Hill, 1960.

McQuigg, B.  The role of education in industry.  Phi Delta Kappan, January, 1980, 61 (5), 324-325.

Milton, O.  Alternatives to the traditional.  San Francisco:  Jossey-Bass, 1972.

Morphet, E.L., & Jesser, D.L. (Eds.).  Designing education for the future (No. 4).  New York:  Citation Press, 1968.

Penland, P.R.  Individual self-planned learning in America.  Washington, D.C.:  Department of Health, Education and Welfare, Office of Education, 1977.

Penland, P.R.  Self-initiated learning.  Adult Education, 1979, 29 (3), 170-179.

Peterson, R.E. and Associates.  Lifelong learning in America.  San Francisco:  Jossey-Bass, 1979.

Pinto, P.R., & Walker, J.W.  What do training and development professionals really do?  Training and Development Journal, July, 1978, pp. 58-64.

Poppenhagen, B.W.  Issues in alternative graduate education.  Alternative Higher Education, Fall, 1979, pp. 3-10.

Poppenhagen, B.W., & Byxbee, W.Jr.  Experiential learning at the graduate level:  a perspective on faculty role and development.  Alternative Higher Education (in press, Winter, 1981).

Schuttenberg, E.M.  An andragogical learning approach to graduate professional education.  Improving College and University Teaching Yearbook.  Corvallis, Oregon:  Oregon State University Press, 1975.

Scriven, M.  The methodology of evaluation.  In B. R. Worthen & J. R. Sanders, Educational evaluation:  theory and practice.  Worthington, Ohio:  Charles A. Jones, 1973.

Shane, H.G.  The educational significance of the future.  Bloomington, Indiana:  Phi Delta Kappan, Inc., 1973.

Siegel, L.  The contributions and implications of recent research related to improving teaching and learning.  In O. Milton & E. J. Shoben, Jr. (Eds.), Learning and the professors.  Athens, Ohio:  Ohio University Press, 1968.

Smith, R.M., Aker, G.F., & Kidd, J.R. (Eds.).  Handbook of adult education.  New York:  Macmillan, 1970.

Somers, N.  Graduate credit for prematriculation experiences.  Alternative Higher Education, Fall, 1979, pp. 32-40.

Steinaker, N.W., & Bell, M.R.  The experiential taxonomy:  a new approach to teaching and learning.  New York:  Academic Press, 1979.

Toffler, A.  A new kind of man in the making.  New York Times Magazine, March 9, 1980, pp. 24-30.

Toffler, A.  Future shock.  New York:  Random House, 1970.

Torbert, W.R.  Learning from experience:  toward consciousness.  New York:  Columbia University Press, 1972.

Tough, A.  The adult's learning projects:  a fresh approach to theory and practice in adult learning (2nd ed.).  Toronto:  The Ontario Institute for Studies in Education, 1979.

Tough, A.  Major learning efforts:  recent research and future directions.  In The adult learner. Washington, D.C.:  American Association for Higher Education, 1978.

Weathersby, R.  Life stages and learning interests.  In The adult learner. Washington, D.C.:  American Association for Higher Education, 1978.

Whitaker, U.G.  Assessors and their qualifications.  In M. Keeton (Ed.), Experiential learning:  rationale, characteristics, and assessment. San Francisco:  Jossey-Bass, 1976.

## APPENDIX

Forms contained in the Appendix may be duplicated in quantity as needed.

Postsecondary Education Internship

PARTICIPANT RÉSUMÉ

Name:_____    Home Tele:_____
        (Last)         (First)       (Middle)

Home Address:_____
             (Street)        (City)      (State & ZIP)

Name of Organization
for Which You Work:_____    Work Tele:_____

Work Address:_____
            (Street)        (City)     (State & ZIP)

### Educational Experience

| Colleges or University Attended (Undergrad.) | Degree Earned | Dates |
|---|---|---|
| | | |

| Colleges or University Attended (Grad.) | | |
|---|---|---|
| | | |

### Professional Experiences

| Name of Organization(s) | Position | Dates |
|---|---|---|
| | | |

Please provide a brief statement of your career goals and how you think the Postsecondary Education Internship will help in pursuing your goals. (Use back of sheet as needed.)

Postsecondary Education Internship

PRELIMINARY LEARNING GOALS FORMULATOR

Instructions:  The purpose of this worksheet is to help you to formulate meaningful learning goals toward which you will work during the Internship experience.  Please formulate goals in three areas:  (A) Cognitive Learning - topics or areas about which you will seek more knowledge; (B)  Affective Learning - areas in which you will further develop feelings, attitudes, and values; (C) Applicative Learning - areas in which you will seek to increase your skills.  You may find it helpful to consult with colleagues or supervisors in completing this worksheet.

A.  Cognitive Learning Goals

1.  For what position(s) in the field of postsecondary education are you most interested in preparing (i.e., counselor, in a ... organization; instructor in a ... institution; administrator in a ... program)?

2.  Considering your prior study and experience, list the topics or the content areas, needed in your field(s) of interest, in which you already have a good deal of knowledge.

3.  Considering your prior study and experience, list the topics or the content areas, needed in your field(s) of interest, in which your knowledge is limited.

4.  Of the items listed above in question A3, place a check by those which you feel have the highest learning priority.

5.  In Column A of the separate form (Appendix C) entitled LEARNING GOALS SELF-EVALUATION FORM - COGNITIVE LEARNING (LGSEF-C), write several cognitive learning goals dealing with the priority areas identified above in questions A3 and A4.

6.  In column B of the LGSEF-C, indicate potential resources or means to attain each goal (i.e., reading, interviews, visitations, discussions, media, observations, projects, etc.).

PRELIMINARY LEARNING GOALS FORMULATOR

B.  Affective Learning Goals

1.  Picture yourself as a practitioner in your field(s) of interest in postsecondary education.  In what aspects of the work would you feel most self-confident?

2.  In what aspects of the work would you feel least self-confident?

3.  What do you feel are your areas of strength in working with people?

4.  What do you feel are your weaker areas in working with people?

5.  Are there any feelings, attitudes, or values that you now hold regarding work and/or other people that you would like to examine more closely?  If so, list them below.

6.  In column A of the separate form, entitled LGSEF-AFFECTIVE LEARN-ING (LGSEF-AF), write several affective learning goals dealing with areas identified above in questions B2, B4, and B5.

7.  In column B of the LGSEF-AF, indicate potential resources or means to attain each goal (i.e., group discussions, value clarification experiences, counseling sessions, sensitivity training, interviews, self-analysis of behavior, peer discussions, feedback sessions, etc.).

C.  Applicative Learning Goals

1.  In what areas related to your field(s) of interest have you already had practical experience?

2.  In what areas related to your field(s) of interest have you had little or no experience?

3.  Of the skills you feel are needed for successful work in your field(s) of interest, in which skills are you already strong?

4.  Of the skills you feel are needed for successful work in your field(s) of interest, in which skills do you need further development?

5.  In column A of the separate form, entitled LGSEF-APPLICATIVE LEARNING (LGSEF-AP), write several applicative learning goals dealing with areas identified above in questions C2 and C4.

6.  In column B of the LGSEF-AP, indicate potential resources or means to attain each goal (i.e., participation, carrying out a project or task, simulated practice, group activities, coaching by others, hands-on experience, etc.).

D.  Internship Learning Design

1.  Considering the cognitive, affective, and applicative learning goals you have set, will it be more feasible for you to select the Learning Contract Option (several different experiences at various levels) or the Learning Project Option (one major project or study which you will conduct)?

2.  If you choose the Learning Contact, what kinds of experiences at the various levels can you engage in?

3.  If you choose the Learning Project, what will be its topic and scope?

Discuss questions D1, D2 and D3 with your Instructor and Field Supervisor as you plan your Internship experiences in detail.

Postsecondary Education Internship

LEARNING GOALS SELF-EVALUATION FORM (COGNITIVE LEARNING)

Based on your analysis of your preparation and interests on the Preliminary Learning Goals Formulator, list below the cognitive learning goals you will strive to achieve during the Internship experience. Complete columns A and B near the beginning of the Internship and columns C and D near the end.

| A. Goals: I plan to gain more knowledge in the following areas: | B. Possible Resources/ Means to attain each goal | C. Attainment (1, 2, 3)* | D. Actual Resources/ Means used to attain each goal |
|---|---|---|---|
| 1. | 1. | 1. | 1. |

* 3 in column C means that the goal has been completely attained; 2 means that the goal has been partially attained; 1 means that the goal has not been attained at all, or only slightly.

Postsecondary Education Internship

LEARNING GOALS SELF-EVALUATION FORM (AFFECTIVE LEARNING)

Based on your analysis of your preparation and interests on the Preliminary Learning Goals Formulator, list below the affective learning goals you will strive to achieve during the Internship experience. Complete columns A and B near the beginning of the Internship and columns C and D near the end.

| A. Goals: I plan to further develop my feelings/ attitudes/values in the following areas: | B. Possible Resources/ Means to attain each goal | C. Attainment (1, 2, 3)* | D. Actual Resources /Means used to attain each goal |
|---|---|---|---|
| 1. | 1. | 1. | 1. |

* 3 in column C means that the goal has been completely attained; 2 means that the goal has been partially attained; 1 means that the goal has not been attained at all, or only slightly.

155

Postsecondary Education Internship

LEARNING GOALS SELF-EVALUATION FORM (APPLICATIVE LEARNING)

Based on your analysis of your preparation and interests on the Preliminary Learning Goals Formulator, list below the applicative learning goals you will strive to achieve during the Internship experience. Complete columns A and B near the beginning of the Internship and columns C and D near the end.

| A. Goals: I plan to increase my skills in the following areas: | B. Possible Resources/ Means to attain each goal | C. Attainment (1, 2, 3)* | D. Actual Resources/ Means used to attain each goal |
|---|---|---|---|
| 1. | 2. | 3. | 4. |

* 3 in column C means that the goal has been completely attained; 2 means that the goal has been partially attained; 1 means that the goal has not been attained at all, or only slightly.

Postsecondary Education Internship

LEARNING EXPERIENCE OVERVIEW LOG SHEET[1]

1.  Name:

2.  Level:
    (3 or 4)

3.  Descriptive Title of Experience:

4.  Short Title (Key words only):

5.  Learning Objectives (What knowledge and skills related to counseling, administration, or instruction are you seeking to learn through this project?):

6.  Experience Objective(s) (What will be achieved as the result of this experience?)

7.  Timeline (What actions will be taken to accomplish the experience and when, approximately, will each action be carried out?):

| Actions | Time |
|---|---|
|  |  |

[1] Use this sheet for levels 3 and 4 experiences only - one sheet per experience. Continue entries on back of sheet as necessary.

Postsecondary Education Internship

LOG ENTRY FORM[1]

1. Name:                                    2. Level:
                                              (1, 2, 3, 4)
3. Title of Experience:

4. Date:                                    5. Duration Covered:

6. Persons Worked With:

7. Summary of Experiences (What was done?):

8. Conceptual Analysis (Insights re counseling, administration, or instruction):

9. Questions, or Topics Needing Further Investigation:

10. Progress Toward Learning Objectives (For Level 3 and 4 Experiences):

11. Progress Toward Experience Objectives (for Level 3 and 4 Experiences):

_____

[1] Use copies of this form for all level experiences. Continue responses on back of sheet as necessary.

Postsecondary Education Internship

INTERNSHIP LOG FEEDBACK FORM

1. <u>Name of Participant:</u>                    2. <u>Date:</u>

2. <u>Name of Reader:</u>

Below are comments and suggestions regarding aspects of your internship
experiences as reflected in your Log entries to date.  Each aspect is
also rated on a 3-point scale (3=strong; 2=average; 1=weak).

| Aspect | Comments and Suggestions | Rating |
|---|---|---|
| A. Ability to set and achieve knowledge- and skill-oriented learning goals | | |
| B. Ability to formulate and achieve work goals | | |
| C. Ability to apply concepts to the analysis of work experiences | | |
| D. Ability to organize and present ideas effectively | | |
| E. Overall use of the Log as a learning tool | | |

Postsecondary Education Internship

ASSESSMENT OF FINAL LOG ENTRIES

1.  Name of Participant:                    2.  Date:

3.  Name of Reader:

Below are comments regarding the final Log entries as they portray your experiences during the internship.  Each aspect is also rated on a 3-point scale (3=strong; 2=average; 1=weak).

| Aspect | Comments | Rating |
|---|---|---|
| A.  Ability to achieve knowledge- and skill-oriented learning goals | | |
| B.  Ability to Achieve Work Goals | | |
| C.  Ability to apply concepts to the analysis of work experience | | |
| D.  Ability to organize and present ideas effectively | | |
| E.  Overall evaluation of Log entries | | |

Postsecondary Education Internship

PROJECT PROPOSAL FEEDBACK FORM

1. Name of Participant:                    2. Date:

3. Name of Reader:

Below are comments and suggestions regarding the Project Proposal and a rating of each Section based on a 3-point scale (3=strong; 2=average; 1=weak).

| Section | Comments and Suggestions | Rating |
|---|---|---|
| A. Statement of Project Goal | | |
| B. Background and Significance of Project | | |
| C. Specific Project Objectives | | |
| D. Definitions, Assumptions, Delimitations | | |
| E. Review of Literature | | |
| F. Project Procedures | | |
| G. Project Time Schedule | | |
| H. Bibliography | | |
| I. Appendixes | | |
| Proposal as a Whole | | |

I

Postsecondary Education Internship

ASSESSMENT OF FINAL PROJECT REPORT

1. Name of Participant:                    2. Date:

3. Name of Reader:

Below are comments regarding the Final Report of the project and a rating
of each Section on a 3-point scale (3=strong; 2=average; 1=weak).

| Sections | Comments | Rating |
|---|---|---|
| J. Project Goal and Actual Procedures<br>  1. General Results<br>  2. Actual Procedures<br>  3. Modified Procedures | | |
| K. Project Results<br>  1. Data re objectives<br>  2. Limitations on interpreting data<br>  3. Summary of results | | |
| L. Conclusions and Recommendations<br>  1. Conclusions<br>  2. Areas for further investigation<br>  3. Suggested changes<br>  4. Follow-up actions<br>  5. Implications | | |
| M. Attachments<br>  1. Summaries of data<br>  2. Other materials | | |
| Report as a Whole | | |

Postsecondary Education Internship

FORMAT FOR REPORTING ORGANIZATIONAL VISITS[1]

1. Participant's name:

2. Organization visited & location:

   Department:
   Division:
   Office:

3. Length of visit:                    4. Date & time:

5. Objective(s) of visit:

6. Summary of visit:

7. Ideas gained:

8. Questions or comments for further study:

9. Additional comments:

---

[1] Use back of sheet for continuing responses as needed.

172

Postsecondary Education Internship

INSTRUCTOR/FIELD SUPERVISOR INTERIM FEEDBACK FORM

<u>To Intern</u>:                                        <u>Date</u>:

<u>From Instructor</u>:
            or
      <u>Field Supervisor</u>:

Based on our working relationship to date, please respond to the following questions and return to me:

1.  Are there particular problems that you are currently facing in your
    Internship that I might help you solve?  If so, what are they?

2.  Are there experiences that you have not yet had that I might help you
    gain?  If so, what are they?

3.  Are there other ways that I might be helpful to you in carrying out
    your Internship?  If so, how?

4.  Is there anything else about the Internship so far that you would like
    to discuss with me at more length?  If so, what is it?

## Postsecondary Education Internship

### PARTICIPANT ASSESSMENT BY INSTRUCTOR

Name of Intern:                                         Date:

Instructor (Signature):

A. Please circle one number under each item with reference to the performance of the Intern named above:

1. Ability to set and achieve cognitive learning goals.

   1(Low)        2           3(Moderate) 4          5              6(High)

2. Ability to apply concepts to work experience:

   1           2           3           4           5           6

3. Ability to organize and present ideas effectively.

   1           2           3           4           5           6

4. Ability to work effectively with people.

   1           2           3           4           5           6

5. Ability to handle stress effectively.

   1           2           3           4           5           6

6. Ability to see and respect others' points of view.

   1           2           3           4           5           6

7. Ability to formulate and attain work goals.

   1           2           3           4           5           6

8. Ability to manage time effectively.

   1           2           3           4           5           6

9. Development of task area skills.

   1           2           3           4           5           6

10. Ability to formulate career goals.

   1           2           3           4           5           6

B. Please comment on your perceptions concerning the preparation and/or potential of the above-named intern for a position in postsecondary education.

1. Areas of strength:

2. Areas needing improvement:

175

Postsecondary Education Internship

FIELD SUPERVISOR FEEDBACK FORM

<u>Name of Intern</u>:                                          <u>Date</u>:

<u>Field Supervisor</u> (Signature):

A.   Please <u>circle one number under each item</u> with reference to the per-
     formance of the Intern named above.

   1.   Ability to organize and present ideas effectively.

     $^1$(Low)         2          $^3$(Moderate) 4          5          $^6$(High)

   2.   Ability to work effectively with people.

     1          2          3          4          5          6

   3.   Ability to handle stress effectively.

     1          2          3          4          5          6

   4.   Ability to see and respect others' points of view.

     1          2          3          4          5          6

   5.   Attainment of work goals.

     1          2          3          4          5          6

   6.   Ability to manage time effectively.

     1          2          3          4          5          6

   7.   Development of practitioner skills.

     1          2          3          4          5          6

   8.   Quality of service to host agency.

     1          2          3          4          5          6

B.   Please comment on your perceptions concerning the preparation and/or
     potential of the above-named Intern for a position in postsecondary
     education.

   1.   <u>Areas of strength</u>:



   2.   <u>Areas needing improvement</u>:

Postsecondary Education Internship

PROGRAM EVALUATION FORM

Part A:   Listed below are the general goals of the Internship.  Circle one number after each goal to indicate the degree to which the goal was achieved for you personally:

1.  To provide participants an opportunity to relate coursework, research, independent study, and simulated experience to actual problems under the direction of an experienced supervisor.

$^1$(Low)        2            $^3$(Moderate)  $^4$        5            $^6$(High)

2.  To make participants cognizant of the responsibilities and duties of the professional personnel in their area of concentration.

1          2          3          4          5          6

3.  To acquaint participants with the on-site resources available to post-secondary education instructors, counselors, administrators, and others.

1          2          3          4          5          6

4.  To provide opportunities for gaining experience in the processes associated with instruction, administration, or counseling in postsecondary education.

1          2          3          4          5          6

5.  To make participants aware of the agencies, both complementary and competing, with which the intern's organization relates.

1          2          3          4          5          6

6.  To develop skills in the task areas normally associated with the roles of administrator, counselor, or instructor.

1          2          3          4          5          6

7.  To become acquainted with the laws, policies, and regulations which govern the operation of the host organization.

1          2          3          4          5          6

8.  To obtain experience in working through and with others toward the realization of common objectives.

1          2          3          4          5          6

9.  To become aware of sources and processes for obtaining necessary data regarding the host organization.

1          2          3          4          5          6

10.  To experience the coordination of the host organization's human and material energies.

1          2          3          4          5          6

# PROGRAM EVALUATION FORM

Part B.  This part deals with your Internship Field Supervisor(s).  <u>Circle one number after each item</u> to express your perception of the Field Supervisor's effectiveness.  If you had more than one major Field Supervisor, use "A", "B", "C", etc., to express your perceptions of each Supervisor:

1. To what extent did your Field Supervisor help you with problems regarding your Internship?

   1(Low)      2      3(Moderate) 4      5      6(High)

2. To what extent was your Field Supervisor's feedback regarding your progress helpful to you?

   1      2      3      4      5      6

3. To what extent was your Field Supervisor available to you for personal consultation?

   1      2      3      4      5 .     6

4. To what extent did you perceive the Field Supervisor's concern for you as a person (not just as an Intern)?

   1      2      3      4      5      6

5. To what extent was the Field Supervisor able to help you find needed resources?

   1      2      3      4      5      6

6. To what extent did the Field Supervisor evaluate your performance effectively?

   1      2      3      4      5      6

Part C:  This part deals with your Internship Instructor.  <u>Circle one number after each item</u> to express your perception of the Instructor's effectiveness:

1. To what extent did your Instructor help you with problems regarding your Internship?

   1(Low)      2      3(Moderate) 4      5      6(High)

2. To what extent was your Instructor's feedback regarding your progress helpful to you?

   1      2      3      4      5      6

3. To what extent was your Instructor available to you for personal consultation?

   1      2      3      4      5      6

## PROGRAM EVALUATION FORM

4.  To what extent did you perceive the Instructor's concern for you as a person (not just an Intern)?

    1(Low)        2          3(Moderate) 4           5           6(High)

5.  To what extent was the Instructor able to help you find needed resources?

    1             2          3           4           5           6

6.  To what extent did the Instructor evaluate your performance effectively?

    1             2          3           4           5           6

7.  To what extent did your Instructor provide you with helpful feedback regarding your written work?

    1             2          3           4           5           6


Part D:  Please provide additional written evaluation of the Internship experience:

Postsecondary Education Internship

FOLLOW-UP SURVEY

Some time ago you completed the Postsecondary Education Internship.  We
are interested in what you have done since then and how you perceive the
Internship at this time.  Please take a few moments to respond to the
items below and return the Survey in the envelope provided.

1.  Have you obtained the kind of position you were hoping for when you
    participated in the Internship? ____Yes; ____No.  If No, are you
    still seeking such a position?   ____Yes; ____No.

2.  What is the title of the position you now hold?

3.  How do you rate the value of the Internship experience?  (Please
    circle one number):

    1           2           3           4           5           6
    (Low Value)             (Moderate Value)                    (High Value)

4.  What aspect(s) of the Internship was of most value to you?

5.  What aspect(s) of the Internship was of least value to you?

6.  Other comments or suggestions re the Internship:

_____
      (Name Optional)

Postsecondary Education Internship

INTERNSHIP PERCEPTION QUESTIONNAIRE[1]

---

Please respond to the items below:

1. Briefly identify the title or nature of your graduate program:

2. Age (please write in): _____

3. Sex: ___Male; ___Female

4. Date (please write in): _____

---

Instructions: On this questionnaire, you are asked to indicate some of your perceptions of your Internship experience. Read the directions for each section of the questionnaire and respond to the items accordingly. Please do not omit any items.

Part A. Next to each of the following statements, write in one number from the Response Key to indicate the degree to which you had each experience during the Internship:

---

Response Key (Part A)
1. I did not experience this
2. I experienced this to a small degree
3. I experienced this to a moderate degree
4. I experienced this to a rather high degree
5. I experienced this to a very high degree

---

1.____    1. At the field site, I learned a lot from listening to other people.

2.____    2. During the Internship, many of my ideas about the way things are done "in the real world" changed significantly.

3.____    3. During the Internship, I found to a greater extent than before that I can "take charge" and "make things happen."

4.____    4. As a result of my Internship experience, I see "theory" and "practice" as being very little related to each other.

---

[1] Ernest M. Schuttenberg, and Brent W. Poppenhagen, Cleveland State University, Cleveland, Ohio 44115, 1979.

## INTERNSHIP PERCEPTION QUESTIONNAIRE

```
                    Response Key (Part A)
          1.  I did not experience this
          2.  I experienced this to a small degree
          3.  I experienced this to a moderate degree
          4.  I experienced this to a rather high degree
          5.  I experienced this to a very high degree
```

5.____    5.  At my field site, I sensed that I was part of a "team."

6.____    6.  During the Internship, I learned to see the points of view of others more readily.

7.____    7.  During the Internship, I perceived myself more as a "professional" than as a "student."

8.____    8.  My Internship experiences helped me to synthesize many of the "pieces" of theory that I had studied.

9.____    9.  At the field site, I found that I was able to be helpful to other people.

10.____   10.  During the Internship, I experienced confusion between being a practitioner and being a student.

11.____   11.  At the field site, I found that if I wanted something to be done correctly, I had better do it myself.

12.____   12.  During the Internship, I was able to make many connections between theory and practice.

13.____   13.  During the Internship, I felt a sense of satisfaction from having an impact on the lives of other people.

14.____   14.  During the Internship, issues became more complex and less "black and white."

15.____   15.  At the field site, I learned better how to cooperate with other people.

16.____   16.  During the Internship, I learned to approach problems from new perspectives.

17.____   17.  During the Internship, I felt increasingly that I was in charge of my own life.

18.____   18.  During the Internship, I realized that problems in the "real world" were more complex than I had thought.

19.____   19.  At the field site, I felt that persons learned from me as I learned from them.

20.____   20.  During the Internship, I learned to be better able to look at situations from other people's points of view.

# INTERNSHIP PERCEPTION QUESTIONNAIRE

> **Response Key (Part A)**
> 1. I did not experience this
> 2. I experienced this to a small degree
> 3. I experienced this to a moderate degree
> 4. I experienced this to a rather high degree
> 5. I experienced this to a very high degree

21. _____    21. At the field site, I learned a lot from the people I worked with.

22. _____    22. During the Internship, my tolerance for ambiguity increased.

23. _____    23. At the field site, I made friends with some of my co-workers.

24. _____    24. The classroom portions of the Internship (at the university) were helpful in interpreting my field experience.

**Part B.** Following are a number of statements that might be made about the Internship experience. Next to each statement write in one number from the Response Key to indicate the strength of your agreement or disagreement with the statement.

> **Response Key (Part B)**
> 1. Strongly disagree    4. Tend to agree
> 2. Disagree    5. Agree
> 3. Tend to disagree    6. Strongly agree

25. _____    25. During the Internship, I relied primarily on myself to plan my learning experience.

26. _____    26. I enjoyed the Internship more than "classroom" courses, because it provided more freedom for me to learn.

27. _____    27. The Internship Guidebook prevented me from designing the kinds of learning projects that I wanted to.

28. _____    28. During the Internship, I felt free to learn in the way(s) I learn best.

29. _____    29. During the Internship, persons at the field site gave me a lot of direction regarding my day-to-day learning experiences.

30. _____    30. When I needed to learn something during the Internship, I sought out the appropriate person(s) or material(s).

31. _____    31. Because of the learning I achieved in the Internship, I feel pride in my accomplishment.

INTERNSHIP PERCEPTION QUESTIONNAIRE

| | Response Key (Part B) | |
|---|---|---|
| 1. Strongly disagree | 4. Tend to agree | |
| 2. Disagree | 5. Agree | |
| 3. Tend to disagree | 6. Strongly agree | |

32.____  32. During the Internship, I was able to get sufficient help in locating learning resources and methods when I needed such help.

33.____  33. The Internship Guidebook was helpful to me in designing my learning projects.

34.____  34. The Internship experiences were very useful to me for career preparation.

35.____  35. During the Internship, I set definite deadlines for myself to complete phases of learning.

36.____  36. During the Internship, I felt that I was learning primarily for myself rather than just "for a course."

37.____  37. During the Internship, I felt that I was almost constantly being evaluated by the Instructor or others.

38.____  38. During the Internship, I learned a great deal about my own way(s) of learning.

39.____  39. Other persons in my Internship group at the university were very helpful to me in planning my learning experiences.

40.____  40. The Internship experience encouraged me to continue learning on my own.

41.____  41. The learning achieved in the Internship repaid the personal effort involved.

42.____  42. During the Internship, I managed my time effectively in order to accomplish learning goals.

43.____  43. The Internship Instructor was of great help to me in planning my learning experiences.

44.____  44. During the Internship, I felt that I had viable options in choosing a variety of ways to learn.

45.____  45. During the Internship, I felt that I was in control of the design and implementation of my learning projects.

46.____  46. As a result of my Internship experiences, I learned better how to learn on my own.

Postsecondary Education Internship

## SUBSCALES OF THE INTERNSHIP PERCEPTION QUESTIONNAIRE

### Decentering Subscale

1. At the field site, I learned a lot from listening to other people.

2. During the Internship, many of my ideas about the way things are done "in the real world" changed significantly.

6. During the Internship, I learned to see the points of view of others more readily.

14. During the Internship, issues became more complex and less "black and white."

16. During the Internship, I learned to approach problems from new perspectives.

18. During the Internship, I realized that problems in the "real world" were more complex than I thought.

20. During the Internship, I learned to be better able to look at situations from other people's points of view.

21. At the field site, I learned a lot from the people I worked with.

24. The classroom portions of the Internship (at the University) were helpful in interpreting my field experience.

### Reciprocity Subscale

5. At my field site, I sensed that I was part of a "team."

9. At the field site, I found that I was able to be helpful to other people.

11. At the field site, I found that if I wanted something to be done correctly, I had better do it myself.*

13. During the Internship, I felt a sense of satisfaction from having an impact on the lives of other people.

15. At the field site, I learned better how to cooperate with other people.

19. At the field site, I felt that persons learned from me as I learned from them.

23. At the field site, I made friends with some of my co-workers.

SUBSCALES

## Holistic Thinking Subscale

4.  As a result of my Internship experience, I see "theory" and "practice" as being very little related to each other.*

8.  My Internship experiences helped me to synthesize many of the "pieces" of theory that I had studied.

12.  During the Internship, I was able to make many connections between theory and practice.

22.  During the Internship, my tolerance for ambiguity increased.

## Sense of Self-Competence Subscale

3.  During the Internship, I found to a greater extent than before that I can "take charge" and "make things happen."

7.  During the Internship, I perceived myself more as a "professional" than as a "student."

17.  During the Internship, I felt increasingly that I was in charge of my own life.

## Self-Directed Learning Approach Subscale

25.  During the Internship, I relied primarily on myself to plan my learning experiences.

27.  The Internship Guidebook prevented me from designing the kinds of learning projects that I wanted to.*

29.  During the Internship, persons at the field site gave me a lot of direction regarding my day-to-day learning experiences.*

40.  The Internship experience encouraged me to continue learning on my own.

46.  As a result of my Internship experiences, I learned better how to learn on my own.

## Self-Directed Learning Skills Subscale

28.  During the Internship, I felt free to learn in the way(s) I learn best.

30.  When I needed to learn something during the Internship, I sought out the appropriate person(s) or material(s).

35.  During the Internship, I set definite deadlines for myself to complete phases of learning.

SUBSCALES

37. During the Internship, I felt that I was almost constantly being evaluated by the Instructor or others.*

42. During the Internship, I managed my time effectively in order to accomplish learning goals.

44. During the Internship, I felt that I had viable options in choosing a variety of ways to learn.

45. During the Internship, I felt that I was in control of the design and implementation of my learning projects.


Rewards of Learning Subscale

31. Because of the learning I achieved in the Internship, I feel pride in my accomplishment.

34. The Internship experiences were very useful to me for career preparation.

36. During the Internship, I felt that I was learning primarily for myself rather than just "for a course."

38. During the Internship, I learned a great deal about my own way(s) of learning.

41. The learning achieved in the Internship repaid the personal effort involved.


Obtaining Relevant Help for Learning Subscale

32. During the Internship, I was able to get sufficient help in locating learning resources and methods when I needed such help.

33. The Internship Guidebook was helpful to me in designing my learning projects.

39. Other persons in my Internship group at the university were very helpful to me in planning my learning experiences.

43. The Internship instructor was of great help to me in planning my learning experiences.

---

\* Scoring of these items should be reversed during computation of total subscale score.

## ABOUT THE AUTHORS

Ernest M. Schuttenberg is an Associate Professor of Education at The Cleveland State University, Cleveland, Ohio. He received his Ed.D. in Educational Administration and Adult Education from Boston University in 1972. Dr. Schuttenberg has taught in high schools and proprietary schools, and he has had several years' experience in management and organizational development in business and industry. He has published several articles in the area of learning theory, educational administration, and adult education.

Brent W. Poppenhagen is Assistant Dean of the College of Education and Assistant Professor of Education at The Cleveland State University, Cleveland, Ohio. He received his Ph.D. in College and University Administration from the University of Wisconsin in 1975. Dr. Poppenhagen has taught and administered at the elementary, secondary, and collegiate levels, and has consulted and taught for several nontraditional degree programs. His publications and research have focused upon alternatives in higher education, adult learning theory, and administrative leadership.

The Cleveland State University, 1983 Euclid Avenue, Cleveland, Ohio 44115.

202